Winning Volleyball

Winning Volleyball

Nicolae Sotir

Translated by **John D. Syer**

National Director,
Scottish Volleyball Association

STANLEY PAUL & CO LTD

3 Fitzroy Square, London W1

AN IMPRINT OF THE HUTCHINSON GROUP

London Melbourne Sydney Auckland
Wellington Johannesburg Cape Town
and agencies throughout the world

First published in Great Britain 1973

This book has been set in Joanna type, printed in Great Britain
on antique wove paper by Anchor Press, and
bound by William Brendon, both of Tiptree, Essex

ISBN 0 09 116330 7

Contents

Introduction

1 The Evolution of Tactics and Technique

Volleyball has evolved from the recreational game of seventy years ago to become an athletic, spectacular, competitive sport. This change came about after the formation of the International Volleyball Federation in 1947 and the subsequent initiation of the first major competitions —the European and the World Championships.

The Russians were the first to show that volleyball could be an important competitive sport. Their appearance at international level completely upset previous conceptions of the game and greatly affected not only skills and tactics but also training methods. Their influence was universal.

Since then the game has greatly progressed, both in quality and extent. The International Volleyball Federation (I.V.B.F.) which originally consisted of only six national Associations, continues to grow. By 1972, twenty-five years after the Federation was founded, one hundred and sixteen countries were affiliated.

The game has become a spectacular sport, if only because players require the physical qualities of strength, speed, control, the ability to relax, technical skill and co-ordination; and the psychological and moral qualities of determination, courage, aggression, selflessness, concentration, team spirit and sportsmanship.

Skills and tactics have evolved along familiar lines. Each time a new element has appeared in the structure of the

attack, it has been quickly parried by a new factor in the
elements of defence, and vice versa. The evolution of the
spike (hitting the ball powerfully down into the opponents'
court) entailed the invention first of the individual and
then of the collective block (the attempt to prevent the
ball crossing the net), as well as a change in the back-court
system of defence.

The effectiveness of the block resulted in a change of
tactics and re-distribution of a team's forces. The old

system of attack involved a division of roles between the six players on court so that three were spikers (and, as such, responsible for hitting the ball into the opponents' court), and three were setters, i.e. were responsible for passing the ball to a position above and close to the net, so that it could be easily spiked.

This system was changed to one in which all six players were spikers when at the net, two of the six doubling this role with that of setting. In this new system, the attack was strengthened by using a back-line setter who 'penetrated' (i.e. ran from the back-line to a position close to the net) as soon as the opponents had served. This allowed any of the three front-line players to attack.

Service has also changed. It is no longer simply the beginning of a rally: it has become a weapon of attack. Service is now used either to score a point directly or to make it difficult for the opposition to build an attack. First, certain teams gained a clear advantage by introducing the powerful windmill and tennis service actions. Then came the floating tennis service. This was used for the first time by the Americans in the 1956 World Championships in

Paris and enabled them to gain many unexpected victories and to finish in fifth place.

In the 1960s, the advent of the Japanese to international play introduced the floating windmill serve, now called the 'Japanese serve'. At first players found it almost impossible to receive the ball, either with a volley (playing the ball on the finger tips above the head) or with a dig (playing the ball on the outstretched forearms).

Service was at first a- very powerful weapon for the Japanese and was one reason for their early supremacy in world-class volleyball. The Japanese women were second at Rio de Janiero (1960), first in the World Championships in Moscow (1962), and first in the Olympic Games in Tokyo (1964). (During the succeeding eight years, however, the Japanese women were beaten back into second place by Russia at every World or Olympic tournament). The Japanese men were eighth in 1960, third in 1964, second at the World Championships in Sofia (1970), and first at the Olympic Games in Munich (1972). Volleyball has become the national sport of Japan.

The Japanese are also responsible for introducing the answer to the floating service. This was their perfection of the dig, which allowed greater control and reduced the hazards of receiving service with a volley. These two major discoveries enabled the Japanese, at quite an early stage, to beat teams which were at that time otherwise superior.

1964 was an important year in the history of volleyball. The game became an Olympic sport and it was in Tokyo that certain new rules, notably one regarding the block, were introduced. The attack had become more powerful than the defence. By allowing the blockers to stretch over the net, the defence was strengthened and, for a few years, the balance was restored.

The introduction of this new rule entailed, as expected, a new development in the attack. The first answer, given by European teams, such as East Germany, Poland and

Bulgaria, was to use very tall players who were able to spike over the block. The tactic was simply to base the attack on a central player, the specialist setter, who set very high balls to the best spikers. This system had some success but made the game less interesting to watch.

The second answer was another innovation by Japan, first seen at the World Championships in Prague in 1966. The Japanese showed that it was possible to make the attack more effective whilst retaining the spectacular nature of the game. This they achieved by introducing extremely fast tactical moves at the net. The ultimate source of the attack, whilst still depending on the effectiveness of the setter, was now largely determined by the spikers calling for the ball as they jumped. A year later, at the European Championships in Turkey, Russia, Poland, Romania, Czechoslovakia, France, Albania, Israel and Holland were already attempting some partial imitation of the Japanese.

The drawbacks of this method of dealing with the strengthened defence became fully apparent in Mexico. Here the Japanese lost two vital matches by three sets to two, having completely bamboozled their opponents during the first two sets. The fast attack with endless dummy spikes by back-line as well as by front-line players was exhausting and it was simply impossible to maintain the original momentum.

However, the Japanese were not discouraged. Their sights were on the Munich Olympics and a carefully ordered progression had been planned. Two years after Mexico, Japan arrived at the World Championships with the tallest team in the competition and demonstrated that they had learnt to vary their own fast attack with the high ball game that had been introduced by the East Europeans.

It is only comparatively recently that emphasis has been placed on developing twelve (not just six plus substitutes) 'complete' players—players who are strong in attack and defence. Height is not enough in itself. The average height for a world-class volleyball player is 1·90 metres, but all players need to be good in the back-court as well as at the net. The duel between Japan and East Germany between 1970 and 1972 was fascinating. The Japanese, so fast in attack and defence, concentrated on height and power and finally arrived in Munich with a block that matched the impenetrable block of the East Germans. The East Germans, on the other hand, demonstrated that they had strengthened their powerful attack and defence at the net by building up a speed and control in the back-court which rivalled that of Japan. East Germany won the 1970 World Championships well but Japan just prevailed at the 1972 Olympics.

Eight years after the rule change on the block, the attack is once more stronger than the defence. At the next Olympic Congress, some other simple but far-reaching rule change will be made to right the situation. Each new development inevitably entails some other compensating move. All sports develop in this way and volleyball is no exception. In any game, the weapons of attack and defence should at least seem to be equal.

2 The Evolution of Training Methods

No progress can be made without training. As the game has evolved, so too have training methods. Indeed, there has been an enormous change in this important area. Totally new training principles and methods of preparation have been adopted. Such changes have affected volleyball, as many other sports, mainly since the Second World War. The last ten years have seen an unprecedented progress in all kinds of sporting performances. Many new achievements would not have seemed humanly possible, two or three decades ago.

If old 'boundaries' are continually being passed, it is due to improved training techniques. The classical method of empirical preparation has been superseded by more rational and scientific training, in which pedagogy, anatomy, psychology, physiology and dietetics all play a part.

Training methods for volleyball are adapted and change continually, according to the general evolution of sports medicine on the one hand and the development of the game's skills and tactics on the other. Any team failing to keep abreast of these changes risks stagnation and even regression, gradually being overtaken by those who were considered less strong. This book attempts to give coaches, teachers, referees and players of volleyball a method of training that is adapted to the present requirements of sport, whether these requirements be of a scientific, technical or tactical nature.

The problem encountered by all those wanting to teach volleyball is to find a correct teaching method that allows a player to learn in the shortest possible time. Obviously it is not easy to reconcile these two requirements.

Anyone starting to learn a team game wants to play at once, without worrying about the correct way of performing the skills involved. If this is allowed for long, it will soon be apparent that the beginner is unable to develop beyond a certain standard. His faulty technique will be holding him back. On the other hand, if a beginner is forced to learn the correct technical skills before he attempts anything else, it will take him three or four years to learn. This method of teaching, in most cases, soon leads the beginner to give up volleyball and to concentrate on a sport that is easier to learn.

Can volleyball be taught both quickly and well? Fortunately it can. If a well thought-out method of training is properly applied, the skills and game of volleyball can be taught in a relatively short period of time.

There has always been discussion as to what constitutes the best way of introducing volleyball to beginners. Both the global and the analytic methods have their advantages and disadvantages.

The global method allows the beginner to play after a very short time, but produces a bad technique that is impossible to correct. The analytic method involves a long and tiresome introductory phase. The beginner learns to perform the skills perfectly in isolation but less well during a game. He becomes an excellent demonstrator but a poor competitor.

If the failings of each of the two traditional methods are considered, a third possibility is clear: a mixture of both.

There is still discussion over the best name for this 'mixed' or 'whole-part-whole' method but there is no doubt that it is effective. Here, the traditional systems are used alternately to teach and perfect each of the skills. The process of alternation is a function of the difficulty and complexity of the skill concerned, the player's own reasons for learning the game, and the length of time available. Each skill must be analysed and the component parts mastered before it is practised in its entirety. There are a number of possible pitfalls in this process and the switch from the analytic to the global method of instruction must be timed correctly if the pitfalls are to be avoided.

The analysis and performance of a given skill should first be made under conditions that are less demanding than the game situation, where rhythm, distance, the rules, etc. all have to be taken into account. This first stage should be relatively short, although some players will need to spend longer at it than others. Once the skill has been learnt correctly, the analytic method is abandoned, except where a bad style has to be corrected.

To gain the full benefit of the mixed method of teaching, the initial instruction in the skills must be complete enough to allow the beginner to take part in a practice game. This does not entail waiting until the players all have learnt to perform the skills perfectly. From the earliest lessons, the players should put the knowledge they have acquired into practice, within a game situation. This helps them to understand the connection between technical skill and tactics, and between the skill in isolation and its use within the context of the game.

To give an example, a one-set practice game can be organised for a group of players who have just learnt to volley. Performance can be improved by ruling that all passes in the game must be made with a volley. Later on, other skills (service, spike, block, etc.) can be analysed, taught and then incorporated one by one into the practice game. It is important always to limit the game to skills that the players have already been taught.

The skills should be introduced in the order in which they will be required by the beginner, progressing from the initial practice game into a full game of volleyball: first the volley, then the service, the dig, the spike, the individual block, the two- and three-man block and finally the roll and dive.

If teaching volleyball is to be structured in this way, a number of ideas about the nature, formation and training of a volleyball team must be changed. The present procedure of getting a group of young people together and immediately entering them in an official competition makes it difficult to instruct the players in the way suggested. Early entry to an official competition requires an immediate knowledge of all the skills. Under these circumstances, it becomes impossible to teach the skills correctly and in the correct order.

Beginners need at least six months' instruction before they enter a competition. This is the time they will require to absorb properly the three basic skills—the volley, the service and the dig. Until they have reached this stage it would be detrimental to their future development for them to attempt competitive volleyball.

If they do play competitive volleyball earlier, two things are likely to go wrong. Firstly, the speed of the game will leave them standing so that they become discouraged and perhaps give up altogether. Secondly, in most cases, the players will acquire ways of playing the ball which are wrong and impossible to correct.

All modern training methods, whether for group or individual sports, stipulate that training should continue throughout the year and not be confined to the four or five months of annual competitions. Unfortunately, these principles are not often applied to club volleyball in West Europe. All too often, when the competitions end, teams disband for the 'dead' season and only get together again a week before the next competition. This makes development to a high standard virtually impossible.

What happens? The skills are not forgotten but the quality of their execution—co-ordination, speed and stamina—deteriorates through lack of practice. The only improvement that the players ever make is made very slowly during the actual competitions.

The rest period should be relatively short, and never exceed two months. Training and matches should continue for the rest of the year. At the start of the new season, there should be a preparation period of about two months, devoted to physical, technical and tactical improvement.

The weekly programme must also connect matches with training. Neither one is any good without the other. Today, all the best teams train several times each week. One or two extra training sessions can only do good, although obviously this will often be difficult to arrange.

Teaching and training methods will continue to be a source of discussion. It is suggested that the above methods be tried. If after several months they have not produced the desired results for any particular club, then the coach concerned will at least be able to make new suggestions based on his own valuable experience. Discussion based on such experience is invaluable. The emergence of a group of creative thinking coaches ensures a major growth of volleyball in the country concerned.

KEY

△	Coach
○ ◑	Players
⌒→	Trajectory of the ball
- - - →	Movement of the players
⟹	Spike
○	Block
△ ⊙	Starting point of the ball

Chapter One: **The Skills**

1 General Observations

The skills of a game may be defined as a group of movements by which, due to its nature and its rules, its objects may best be attained.

The particular importance of the skills of volleyball derives from the special nature of the rules. There are several marked differences between volleyball and the other team ball games (handball, football, basketball, rugby, etc.). In volleyball,

(i) The ball may not be caught or held, and all passes are very short.

(ii) The number of passes between members of a team is limited (to three).

(iii) A net separates two areas of play.

(iv) A relatively small court (9m. by 9m.) is defended throughout by six players. The players have to control the ball at speed, often from awkward unbalanced positions.

(v) The fact that there is no bodily contact with opponents might give the impression that it is easier to perform the various skills than it is in other team sports. This is not the case, since freedom from interference is balanced by rules governing performance of the skills. Any technical mistake (e.g. handling faults such as a double-touch or a carry, net faults or foot faults, etc.)

made by one of the players penalises the whole team. (The team loses a point or service.)

(vi)   The ball must not touch the ground.

(vii)   The ball must be returned over the net into the opponents' court, on or before the third touch.

These factors are psychologically important and often account for the apparently inexplicable way that a team will suddenly lose its confidence. This can happen when a number of faults are made in quick succession. The coach, who is allowed two times out and six substitutions in each set, often has to interrupt the match or change his players: in doing so he attempts to calm his team or to rest one of his players.

Rotation is another peculiarity of volleyball. Each player in the team must occupy each of the positions on court in turn. He is thereby required to adopt each of the various roles of the game—spiker, blocker, back-court defender, setter and server. The volleyball player must be polyvalent and master all the skills. He should not specialise. If he does, the opposition will take advantage of his weaknesses.

A player cannot defend or attack without the help of the other players in his team. If the players are not equally good and able to play as one unit, the team will be unable to do anything constructive. The best player will be unable to benefit from his greater ability. If the rest of the players are inept, the ball will never be passed to him properly. For a game to be worth watching, it must consist of long, fast rallies. These will only come when all the players are non-specialist and are technically and physically equipped to perform all the skills of the game.

An analysis of the basic skills shows they are not movements that are normally made in everyday life. They are unusual and made under unusual circumstances—often when turned the wrong way or when off-balance. The movement to the ball, the position under the ball before playing it, and the skills themselves are, for instance, quite different from those involved in handball or basketball.

Learning all the skills of volleyball, though difficult, is indispensable. In fact, this is the real problem for the beginner. To understand better what is involved, one need only move around in the way a player has to move during a game—make a set pattern of skill movements for four or five minutes—to realise the problem. One sees that, at the first attempt, it is both very difficult to make the movements correctly and extremely tiring.

It is clear that, given the nature of the rules and the difficulty in performing the skills correctly, beginners should not be left to fend for themselves. If the skills are to be performed correctly and creatively in the game situation, they must be acquired through a course of proper instruction.

2   Classification of the Skills

The continued evolution of volleyball makes it necessary to alter somewhat the old classification of the skills. Given the various positions, movements and skills involved, this would seem to be the best classification: (i) Basic positions (ii) Movement on court (iii) The volley (iv) The dig (v) The service (vi) The spike (vii) The block and (viii) The dives, back-rolls and side-rolls.

Certain of the skills are used both in attack and in defence —for instance, the various positions and movements on court. Other elements are specifically used in the spike or service (e.g. the arm action). The block is used exclusively in defence, although at times it is an effective counter-attack.

The eight basic skills can be divided into the simple and the complex. The simple skills are performed from an initially balanced position, e.g. the service and the block. The complex skills are a succession of simple movements which depend on the ball, the members of one's own team, and one's opponents. Each basic skill has several variations.

A team composed of players who can perform each skill in various ways will be able to play at a high level.

Each basic skill and its variants should be taught first by verbal analysis and then by practical demonstration.

3 Basic Positions

A player must move into a correct position before playing the ball. This is true of most team sports but especially of volleyball. Since the rules do not allow the ball to be held, it is impossible to change position whilst playing the ball. The basic positions are high, middle and low. They differ,

1
Left:
High
position

2
Right:
Middle
position

3
Left:
Low position

4
Right:
Position for
service
reception
or dig

according to how far the knees are bent, and in the position of the arms.

In the middle position, the legs are slightly bent. The feet are the distance of the shoulders apart and placed one in front of the other, weight being equally distributed. The trunk leans slightly forwards, the arms are bent, the hands are cupped and held at chest-height. A variation of this position is increasingly used by players when receiving service with a dig. In this, the feet are placed level with each other and further apart. The arms are also further apart and are held at waist height.

Given the importance of balance and orientation, it is essential that the player learns the various positions. He must maintain the middle position as he moves on court, throughout the point. It is difficult to move in the low position: this should only be adopted just before passing or retrieving the ball.

It is easy to learn the basic positions. Any mistake should be corrected immediately. The following mistakes are fairly common. (i) Poor balance, weight not being equally distributed; (ii) The trunk too far forwards so that the head is strained backwards; (iii) The feet too far apart, making it impossible to move quickly.

It is important to link the positions with movement, right from the start. These movements must be learnt and improved simultaneously. The best way to teach the movements is to explain, demonstrate and then ask the players to try. Having moved from one place to another, the players should complete the movement by straightening their legs and finally by making a complete 'shadow' volley action.

4   Movement on Court

In the past, the importance of correct movement on court has been neglected. Nowadays it is recognised that control in performing the various skills depends on rapid balanced movement, prior to playing the ball. Any delay in moving to the ball will affect the degree of precision obtained and may cause a handling fault. Every shot requires some adjustment of the body in relation to the trajectory of the approaching ball, both in attack and in defence.

The player's main problem is to be fast and well-balanced whilst keeping the basic stance. Volleyball involves stepping forwards, backwards and sideways, skipping sideways, jumping and sprinting. These movements are all used in other sports, in common with volleyball. The side-skip is particularly suited to volleyball since it allows almost perfect balance.

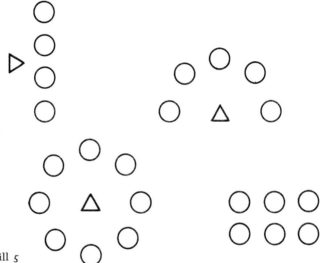

Drill 5

The following are drills for teaching the various movements on court.

(i)   Players step one pace forward and adopt the 'middle' position. This is repeated but moving into the position from one pace backwards, one pace to the right and one pace to the left.

(ii) As above, but taking two or three paces into the position—first at walking pace, then at speed.

(iii)   Players move backwards and forwards, stopping in the middle position when a signal is made. Both oral and visual signals can be used.

(iv)   Side-skipping. Forwards and backwards, as in drill ii.

(v)   As drill iv, only making changes of direction.

(vi)   Players in pairs. One moves and adopts one of the three basic positions. His partner copies him.

(vii) The same movements practised competitively. (e.g. relay races, etc.)

Other drills can be used that require several kinds of movement. Every movement or group of movements should end in a correct position and a 'shadow' volley. The players can best learn to move in the 'medium' position by holding a medicine ball, basketball, football or volleyball, as they move.

The same drills can be used to improve the movement of experienced players, by conducting them at a higher speed. The coach must then control the number of repetitions, the distance to be covered, the duration of each drill and the periods of rest between drills.

When a player is able to adopt a correct position, move rapidly and re-adopt that position, he is ready to learn the volley.

5   The Volley

The volley is the action of receiving and passing the ball. This action must be performed so naturally that its two elements appear to be one. This is why the skill is difficult, both for the beginner and for the player who is trying to improve.

Every training session should include drills for practising the volley. The coach or teacher should always insist on the volley being performed correctly. It is almost impossible to correct a bad style once it has been adopted.

All parts of the body are involved. The action must be continuous, co-ordinated and controlled. If it is performed in any other way, a variety of mistakes can occur (e.g. the ball played at full stretch, the legs stiff, the arms stretched or not moving into the ball with the rest of the body, a lack of co-ordination between the various parts of the body, etc.). The ability ·to gauge the ball's trajectory is also of prime importance. This must be done if the player is to move correctly under the ball.

The volley is taught first without the ball, the action being performed after correct footwork and the adoption of a correct stance. When the ball is introduced, the players must still move a few steps into position before volleying. This teaches them to gauge variations in the flight of the ball. Such judgement is critical. Most beginners find it difficult, however, especially in awkward or complex situations, such as passing the ball without pause between two or more players. The following progression of training drills will help.

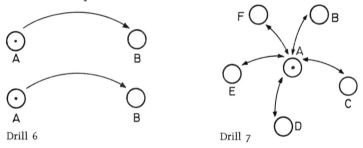

Drill 6   Drill 7

Stage one: The first drills are performed with a medicine ball (the volume of a volleyball and weighing 800 grams).

In drills 6 and 7, player A passes the medicine ball to players, B, C, D, E and F. He throws it fairly high, directly above them, so that they can catch it without moving. As they catch the ball, the players naturally adopt the correct basic stance for volleying. When they pass the ball back to player A, they use the volley action that they have already learnt. Any player still not making the right action should be corrected.

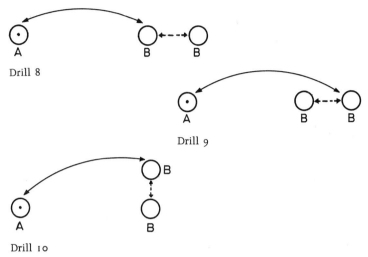

Drill 8

Drill 9

Drill 10

Stage two: The next drills involve moving slightly, before receiving the ball. Drill 8 involves moving forwards, drill 9 backwards and drill 10 sideways. In each drill, player A throws the medicine ball so that player B can move into the correct position under the ball, catch it, and return it with a volley action. At first the three drills should not be mixed: player B should know in advance where the ball is to be thrown.

Later, the distances can be increased, so that B has to move two or three paces before catching the ball. A can also vary the direction in which he throws the ball, at random.

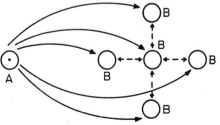

Drill 11

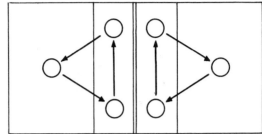

Drill 12

Drill 12 is the same as drill 11, with the difference that three players take part instead of two—the ball still being caught.

Drill 13 is a game between two groups of four, five or six players on an ordinary court. The game is played without service. The medicine ball is passed from one player to another (two or three times on each side of the net) and across the net to the other team. The drill can be made into a game by penalising faults and counting points. Catching

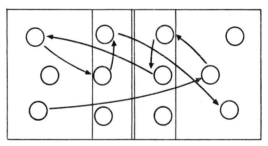

Drill 13

the ball in a bad position, taking a step whilst holding the ball, touching the net, etc., will be counted as faults. The drill teaches the players to judge the flight of a ball and to take into account the area of the court and the net.

Stage three: Drills 6 to 11 are repeated with a volleyball, instead of the medicine ball. When a player has assimilated the correct action, he is ready to volley properly, without catching the ball.

This introduces new problems. The first is orientating

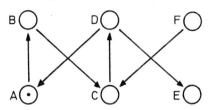

Drill 14

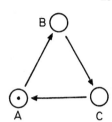

Drill 15

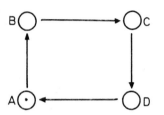

Drill 16

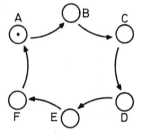

Drill 17

the body in relation to the trajectory of the ball—firstly when receiving a pass and secondly when making one.

Drills 14 to 17 involve passing the ball in various patterns which gradually become more difficult. By mastering these drills the player gradually learns to cope with changes of direction and orientation. N.B. The player who receives the ball must position himself in relation to the player to whom he is going to pass. For example, in drill 15, A must be facing B at the moment the ball from C reaches him.

From this point, drills can be introduced which involve moving both before and after volleying.

Drill 18

Drill 19

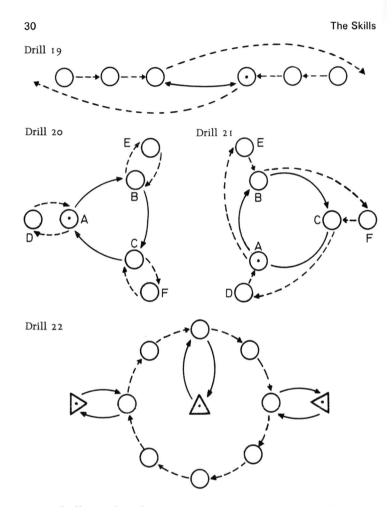

Drill 20

Drill 21

Drill 22

In drill 22, the players move round in a circle. The three feeders, one in the centre and two outside, each have a ball and pass it to each player as he moves by. The player must move into the basic volleying position, stop and volley the ball correctly and accurately back to the feeder.

In drill 23, the player volleys the ball against a wall, varying both the height and speed of the ball so that he is forced to move in order to receive and play it again correctly.

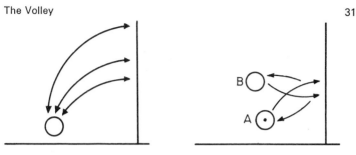

Drill 23   Drill 24

Drill 24 is the same, only with two players. Drill 25 is very much more difficult. One player stands behind the other but they change places after each volley.

When a player can volley correctly and control the ball in different circumstances, he will have acquired the basic correct reactions. The next step is to improve his ability to watch the ball by making his partner or his opponent move.

In drill 26, player A volleys so that B must move to receive the ball. A must volley the ball precisely to any position named by B.

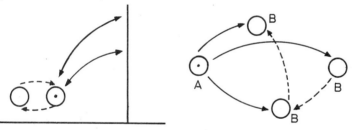

Drill 25   Drill 26

In drill 27, the players should wear jerseys of differing colours or numbers. B always volleys to R, who volleys to Y, who volleys to G, who volleys to B. At first the players don't move but then they move each time, after volleying.

In drill 28 players A and B volley the ball to each other as they move down the length of the court. The coach complicates the drill by telling the players they must stay on court, not touch the net, etc.

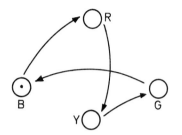

Drill 27

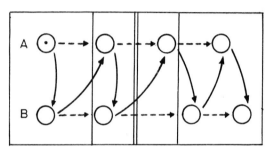

Drill 28

Whilst working on this aspect, other drills can be introduced which accustom the player to the size of the court and the positions of the net. This, in fact, is the first tactical application of the skills.

Drill 29 is to practise volleying at the net.

Drills 30 and 31 demand precision in height and distance, drill 31 involving the same factors but also requiring the players to move before they volley.

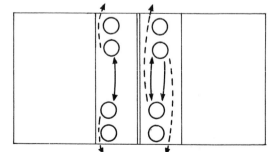

Drill 29

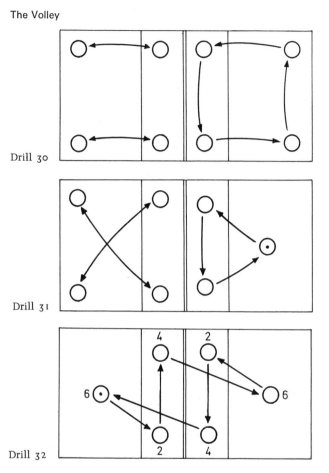

Drill 30

Drill 31

Drill 32

Fig. 32 shows a drill for a minimum of six players (three against three), in which the players do not change positions.

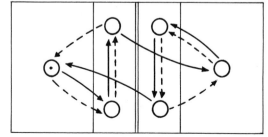

Drill 33

In drill 33, the ball is played to the same positions but the players move, following their volleys.

It is easy to invent more drills of this kind. The main thing is to remember what they are for and to introduce them in the right order. As the players improve, the drills should become increasingly complex. The players gradually learn to move into position from which they can produce a correct, controlled volley, in any situation.

Once this has been achieved, the player must learn two other types of volley: the overhead pass and the jump volley. The *overhead pass* differs from a normal volley in that the legs are further apart, to ensure better balance, and the ball is played directly above the player's head. The player must rise into the ball and must watch the ball as it travels up and behind him.

In drill 34, A volleys to B who volleys overhead to C, who volleys a long pass back to A.

Drill 35, the same drill, only as soon as he has made an overhead pass, B turns to face that direction.

Drill 36, the same as drill 35 but with more players. Each player turns after he has volleyed so that the drill can be repeated. The players at the end of the line start the drill by turning and volleying overhead to the next player.

Drill 37: Player A volleys the ball high against the wall. B moves under the ball and returns it to A with an overhead volley.

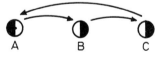
Drill 34

Drill 35

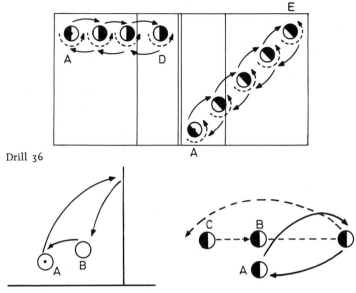

Drill 36

Drill 37   Drill 38

Drill 38 : Player A volleys the ball high and to the left of B. B runs under the ball, turning and returns the ball overhead to A. B then moves to the back of the queue and the drill is repeated with the next player, C.

Drill 39 : Player 6 passes to 2, who passes to 3, who makes an overhead pass to 4, who returns the ball to 6. The players change places by following the ball. (The drill is for five players, the fifth replacing player 6 as he runs to replace player 2.)

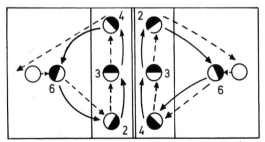

Drill 39

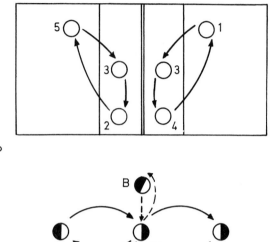

Drill 40

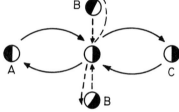

Drill 41

Drill 40. The same drill but without changing places and with the ball starting from position 1. This requires player 3 to alter the trajectory of the ball, which is more difficult.

Drill 41. A feeds the ball to B so that he must move sideways before volleying overhead to C. B must then move to the other side, turn to face the ball coming from C and volley overhead to A. Passing should be continuous for forty-five seconds to a minute.

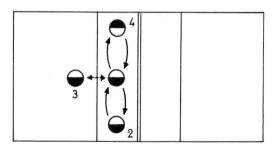

Drill 42

Drill 42. The same but at the net. Player 3 moves out to the 3 metre line to receive the ball. Since this drill is very tiring, players 2 and 4 can be instructed to volley once above their own heads before passing.

The *jump volley* is another type. It is difficult to perform well and should only be used by experienced players. It is generally used for tactical reasons but can also be employed in a difficult situation to correct an error of timing. In the first case the player jumps square to the net but turns in the air to face the direction in which he volleys. In the second case the performance of the action depends on the situation. The jump volley must be learnt and practised so that it can be used when the occasion demands. It should not be used indiscriminately because of the risks involved.

The ball is played from a well-balanced vertical jump, legs straight, arms stretched upwards, elbows bent and hands held level with the forehead. The ball is projected by the arms and fingers, at the moment when the player is at the height of his jump.

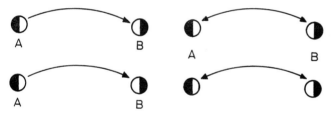

Drill 43   Drill 44

Drill 43. Two players stand 3 or 4 metres apart. A volleys the ball with his feet on the ground. B returns it with a jump volley.

Drill 44. As in Drill 43, only both players jump volley.

Drill 45. Players in two lines jump volley across the net, going to the end of the line on the opposite side after volleying.

Drill 46. Jump volley across the net, in pairs.

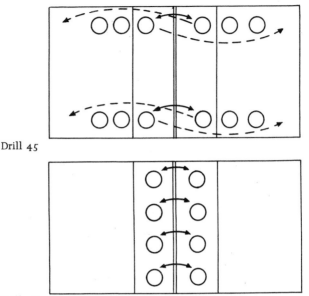

Drill 45

Drill 46

Drills 29 to 33 can be adapted to practising the overhead jump volley, a shot that is much more difficult.

There is one other type of volley—the *side volley*—but its use is limited and it is difficult to perform without fouling.

The forward volley is therefore only one of several types of volley but it is important that the various types of volley are introduced to the beginner stage by stage, with drills that are presented in a correct order. The drills already mentioned are designed for beginners and are relatively simple, in that they do not require much physical effort. Once the beginners have reached a certain level of proficiency, there is no point in repeating the same drill, because it will no longer help the player to improve.

At this point other training problems must be considered. Firstly, a way must be found to improve the player's stamina: no matter how tired he may be, he must be able to repeat the same skills throughout a match, with the same degree of co-ordination, precision and intelligence. Secondly, by using more complex drills, the training must get gradually closer to the game situation: technique must be related to tactics.

Stamina can be improved by circuit training but there are other ways too. Certain complex drills can improve stamina and skill performance at one and the same time. With this type of drill, great attention must be paid to duration, speed, distance, related actions, the number of players taking part, etc.

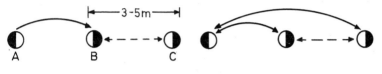

Drill 47   Drill 48

Drill 47. Player A volleys to a point in front of him. B volleys back to A, runs back three to five metres and returns to the same position to play the next volley. The drill should last for one to three minutes.

Drill 48. Same as drill 47 but B volleys to A twice as often: alternately from the original position and the point to which he runs.

Drill 49. Same as drill 47, but B runs to one side.

Drill 50. Same as drill 48, but B runs up to 7 metres to one side.

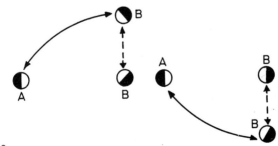

Drill 49

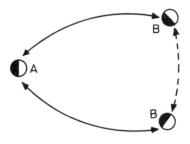

Drill 50

These four drills (47–50) all involve moving a certain distance repeatedly, for a determined length of time. Another element, change of rhythm, can be introduced by varying the flight of the ball: high balls will produce a slow rhythm, low balls will speed it up. If the drills are performed on the court in relation to the net, greater precision will be required.

Complex drills, close to the game situation, can be introduced once several skills have been learnt. For example, a drill closely resembling a game can be made up once the players have been taught to volley, serve and receive service. With this sort of drill it is easy for players to improve stamina and skill, whilst gaining an appreciation of the tactical objectives of the game.

6   The Dig

This skill has been used notably by the Czechs, for more than twenty years. In this time, however, the technique has changed radically. Since the Japanese first demonstrated that the dig could be used to receive all types of service (notably the floating variety), the skill has been adopted by teams throughout the world, both for receiving service and recovering spikes. The elements of the dig are easily learnt but constant practice is required to attain precision in its use.

From the basic stance already described, keeping his arms straight, the player brings his hands together in front of him. He then turns them back at the wrists, so as to lock his elbows. The ball is played on the flat inner surface of the fore-arms.

As with the volley, the action involves the whole body moving into the ball. At the same time a slight independent movement of the arms is used for direction and control. The harder the ball that has to be received, the less movement there will be into the ball on reception. As with the volley, the player must always be positioned beneath the ball at the moment in which it is played.

The drills used for the volley may be used to teach the dig but the distance between players should be increased to at least 9 metres. The drills should also include the reception of service and the recovering of spikes.

Drill 51. The players are in pairs, 9 or 10 metres apart. A throws the ball, overarm, at B, who receives it with a dig. A may obtain a steeper angle by standing on a chair; he should vary the length of his throw. The drill can be repeated, with A serving the ball (using a tennis or floating service) instead of throwing it.

Drill 52. Player A serves from behind the back-line to B, who stands 7 or 8 metres beyond the net. B receives the ball with a dig, directing it to a point within the attack zone.

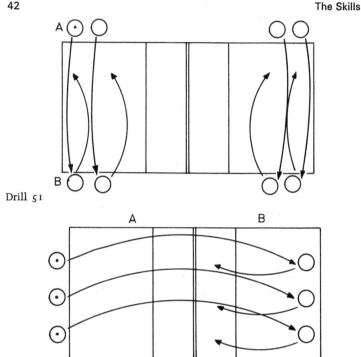

Drill 51

Drill 52

7 Service

Service is the easiest skill to learn. Though largely a matter of physical ability, the importance of precision and dependability should be stressed. Untempered strength results in many mistakes.

Underarm services are the easiest to perform. There are two types, the frontal and the lateral. For the first, the player stands square to the net, his left foot forward if he is right-handed, (right foot forward if he is left-handed), legs slightly bent. If he is right-handed, he holds the ball in his left hand, his right arm held slightly behind him, hand cupped and fingers pressed together.

As the ball leaves his left hand, his striking arm swings

forward. His hand hits the lower back part of the ball, in front of him at waist-height. At the same time, he straightens his front leg and trunk, bringing his back leg forwards and moving into position on court. He must avoid the following mistakes: (i) placing his feet wrongly; (ii) his striking arm being too bent; (iii) hitting the ball either too near or too far from his body (see Fig. 53).

A few simple drills help the beginner to learn to throw the ball up and hit it correctly.

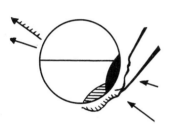

Fig. 53

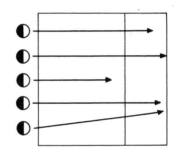

Drill 54

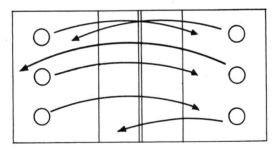

Drill 55

Drill 54. The players serve at a wall, standing 9 metres in front of it.

Drill 55. When the time comes to practise serving over the net, girls and very young players should start serving from a point within the court, gradually serving from further back until they can get the ball over the net from the proper service area.

As soon as the player can serve consistently into the opposite court, from the service area, emphasis is put on precision.

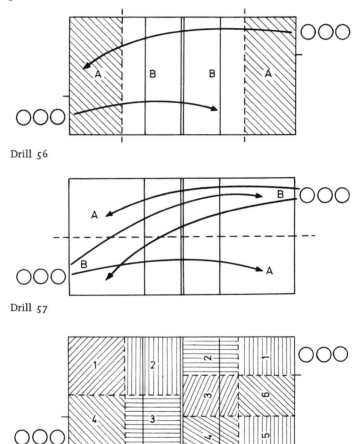

Drill 56

Drill 57

Drill 58

Drill 56. The court is divided into zones and each server must serve the balls into a particular zone.

Drill 57. The same drill but different zones.

Drill 58. Gradually the number of zones is increased to six.

The second type of underarm service, the lateral service, is made from almost the same stance but the player stands with his shoulders perpendicular to the net. The striking arm swings forward across the body. The action is practised in the same way as the other type of underarm serve.

There are four types of overarm service: the strong tennis serve, the floating tennis serve, the strong windmill serve and the floating windmill serve. Nowadays the strong services are rarely used, due to the high proportion of mistakes that they entail—even when performed by the most experienced players. Most teams therefore use the floating services almost exclusively. They are very much more consistent and, in the end, are more effective.

For the strong tennis serve, the player begins from a well-balanced position, with one foot in front of the other and the shoulders parallel to the net. As he throws the ball in the air, his striking arm swings behind his head, elbow held high, hand cupped and shoulders turned away from the net. Then his weight swings forward. He hits the ball at a point higher than his head and directly above his front foot. His back leg swings forward as he hits the ball, so that he is already moving to take up his position on court.

The player adopts the same initial position for a floating tennis serve. The serve is made without effort and without using the trunk. The ball is hit centrally, with the heel of the hand. The hand may be either open or closed. The arm and hand action is halted abruptly at the moment the ball is hit. The main object is to avoid making the ball spin: if it spins it will not float in the air. The same drills can be used to practise the tennis serves as those given for the underarm serves.

The strong windmill serve is more difficult to master. The initial stance is the same as for the lateral underarm serve. As he throws the ball in the air, the player swings his trunk and back leg sideways and, turning away from the court, leans down and extends his serving arm. From this point, his arm swings up and his whole body straightens. He hits the ball at a point above his head and in front of his body, with the full force of the windmill action.

The windmill service depends largely on the ball being thrown up correctly. If the ball is thrown too near to the body or too far to one side or in front, the arm-swing and the position of the body will automatically change. The ball will then be hit incorrectly. If the throw is wrong, it is better to let the ball fall, without touching it, and start again.

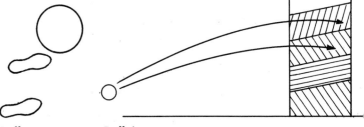

Drill 59   Drill 60

Since this service is difficult, the action should first be practised without the ball. The player should then practise the throw. If the ball is thrown correctly, it should fall on the ground beside the front foot (see Fig. 59). Ideally, the arm-action should then be practised by aiming at a ball that is hung at the right height from the ceiling. If this cannot be arranged, another player can stand on a chair and hold the ball. Great attention should be paid to the correct swing of the arm, and the straightening of the trunk and legs.

Later, the player should practise serving at a wall, aiming at different heights, from a distance of 5 to 7 metres. (See Drill 60.) After this, the player can serve over the net, at first from about 4 metres away and then gradually increasing the distance. *The strength of the service is of no importance until the action has been properly learned.* Finally drills for improving precision are introduced. Since the strong windmill service is necessarily less precise than other services, there is no point in dividing the court into more than four zones.

1

2

3

4

5

6

The floating windmill service, see page 47, usually known as the Japanese serve, is one of the most common in the modern game. It is normally performed from the same initial stance as the strong windmill serve, although there are many different individual styles. A study of the Japanese national women's team showed that the players had their own individual ways of performing the service.

The most common method is as follows. From the initial stance the player almost turns his back to the net. Even the hand holding the ball is behind the body, towards the side of the striking arm. As the body straightens, the player throws the ball much lower and nearer to the body than in the strong windmill serve. At the same time, the other arm loosely extended and the rest of the body swing quickly on to the ball. The impact is relatively slight. The ball is usually hit with the flat of the hand but, as with the tennis floater, there is no follow through and the ball is hit so that it does not spin. The drills used for the underarm services can also be used to practise the Japanese serve.

Other types of service exist but are not greatly used, for example the pushed serve, the high (Czech) serve, etc.

The player has to spend a great deal of time practising service, if his serve is to be precise, consistent and attacking. To help maintain the players' interest, practice can take the form of a competition. Several services, anything from five to fifty, can be made in succession, with a system of points in operation. At the same time, to keep the players under pressure physically, so that they are serving in conditions similar to a match, they can be asked to volley, to change direction, to dive or to block between services. If this is not done, the situation is unreal since service alone requires very little physical exertion.

1

2

3

4

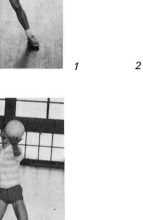

5

6

8   The Spike

The spike is the most complex skill of all and presents the beginner with a number of problems. Despite this, it is the skill which the beginner finds the most attractive. In order to avoid mistakes which later become impossible to correct, it is best to teach the spike analytically, making a careful study of each part of the action separately. These parts are the run-up, the jump, movement in the air, hitting the ball and landing.

The run-up is normally of three accelerating paces. It is determined by the height of the ball and its position in relation to the net. It should be made as perpendicularly to the net as possible, so that the spike may be made in any direction. The final step is the most important. It must be both longer and faster. The player must watch the ball throughout the run-up.

The speed gained by the run-up must be converted into a high vertical jump. The player should avoid stepping heavily on the ground, since this would create an opposite force to the one required. On the last pace, the foot opposite to the spiking arm is forward, heel on the ground first, followed by the sole of the foot. The other foot must on no

account move in front but, with the weight on the front
foot, the other skims along the ground and the player
jumps off both feet at the moment they are side by side.
The arms are swung backwards to check the forward movement. At the moment of take-off, the body is leaning
forwards, weight still on the foot that was in front and the
arms are fully extended, parallel to the ground behind the
player.

The power of the take-off (see photo opposite) comes
from the thrust of the player's legs helped by the arms,
which are swung forwards and upwards. As the player
leaves the ground, his body is relaxed, his arms still sweep-
ing upwards in front of him. The non-striking arm must
swing up at least as far as the player's face, causing the
shoulder to rise, the trunk to stretch and reaching a
position from which it can lead the whole upper half of
the body into the forward striking action, thereby increasing
the power of the spiking arm. Meanwhile the spiking arm
continues upwards, the elbow pointed forwards.

The ball is struck above its horizontal axis with the palm
of the hand. The player's fingers are closed together, bent
slightly forward, so as to exactly cover the top of the ball.
The wrist is locked as the ball is hit but loosened immediately afterwards, so that the ball can be directed downwards. The strength of the spike depends on the speed of the
arm.

The player lands on both feet (toes, soles, heels) and
his legs bend. His landing must be supple and well-
balanced, allowing him to play the ball again immediately
(e.g. make a dive, a volley or a second spike). The rule that
allows a player to make a second consecutive touch after
blocking increases the importance of landing well.

The above analysis of the various elements of the spike
shows the complexity of the skill. Each element is important
and an error in the performance of any one of them will
reduce the effectiveness of the spike. However, the most

frequent cause of a bad spike is an incorrect approach. The
run-up must begin at the right moment and must be made
so that the jump is on the correct spot. In order to judge the
run-up correctly, the player must make a true assessment of
the flight of the ball. After leaving the setter's hands, the ball
has a parabolic flight. Since the ball will fall symmetrically
to its upward path, it is impossible to gauge its downward
path whilst it is still rising. This means that the player must
not begin his run-up until after the ball has reached the
height of its flight.

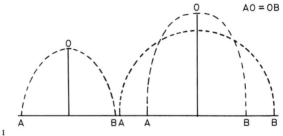

Fig. 61

Each element of the spike should be taught in turn and
first be practised without the ball. The various elements can
then be strung together and the ball should be used. Accent
must be laid on the co-ordinated rhythm of the complete
action.

The first part of the spike to be learnt is the take-off. The
player, from the basic stance, takes one large pace on to his
heel, bends his knee, transfers his weight on to this front
foot and swings the rest of his body forwards as if to take-off.
The movement should be made slowly at first: a long step
with the left foot, followed by a short step with the right
(the opposite for the left-handed spiker). After repeating this
slowly several times, the movement can be speeded up and
the jump added, with the arms swinging right through.

Another pace can be added—a short pace followed by the
long stride. The jump must be vertical and, to help the
player in this, he can practise running-up and jumping

in front of the net, a line on the floor, or the wall. A third
pace is then added to complete the run-up: two short paces
and one large one (Fig. 63).

Drill 64. Practise the spike action, without the ball, at the
net.

Drill 65. The coach throws the ball. The player makes a
normal run-up and jump but catches the ball in mid-air.
Any players unable to do this should pause after the
run-up before jumping.

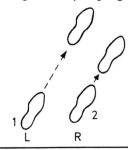

Fig. 62

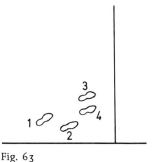

Fig. 63

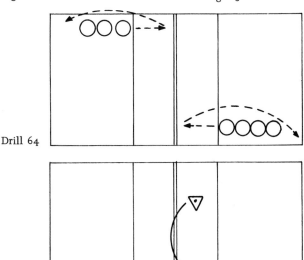

Drill 64

Drill 65

Drill 66. Practise the take-off action and the spiking action without the run-up or the jump, i.e. deep knee bend, body leaning forwards, arms back then swing the arms right through and make the spike action.

Drill 67. Same drill, adding the jump.

Drill 68. Same as before but adding the run-up.

Drill 69. (i) Hold the ball at arms length at shoulder height and perform the spiking action, hitting the ball on to the ground. (ii) Throw the ball up before hitting it.

Drill 69   Drill 71

Drill 70. Same drill but jumping. Drill 71. Drills 69 and 70, hitting the ball so that it bounces back off the wall. Repeated without pausing.

Drill 72. A drill to teach the player to raise his non-spiking arm. Holding a tennis ball in each hand, he runs up to the net and jumps. At the height of his jump he throws the two balls over the net: first the ball held in his non-spiking hand and then the other. For this drill the net can be lowered slightly.

Drill 73. With the net slightly lowered, the player stands just behind it, throws up the ball and hits it over—first without jumping and then jumping.

Drill 74. The coach stands on the opposite side of the net to the players and throws the ball across the net. The player runs in, jumps and spikes.

Drill 75. The coach stands in position 3 and throws the balls to the player, who is in position 4. The net is gradually raised as the player's spike becomes increasingly co-ordinated.

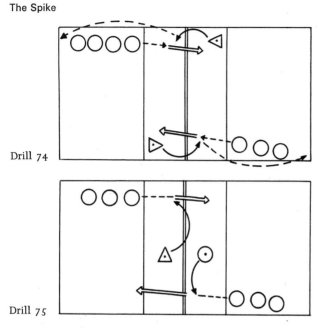

Drill 74

Drill 75

Drill 76. The same, only the coach volleys the ball to the player and the net is gradually raised to the correct height. If the player is unable to judge the flight of the ball, the coach must tell him when to run-in. He should also correct every mistake as it occurs, so that it is not repeated.

To begin with, when learning to spike, the power of the shot is of little importance. Above all, the player must make sure that he performs the skill correctly. Once he can do this, he should learn to place the ball.

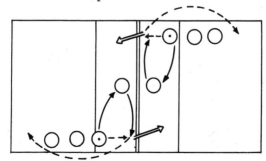

Drill 77

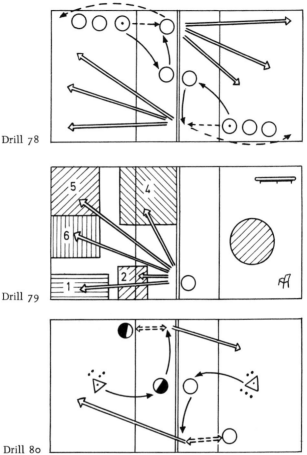

Drill 78

Drill 79

Drill 80

Drill 77. Practise spiking from position 2. Drill 78. Vary the direction of the spikes. Drill 79. Mark out zones on the opposing court. (Eventually targets can be placed within the zones.) The player must hit the ball into one or other zone, according to the coach's directions. Points can be awarded according to the difficulty of placing the ball in a particular zone.

Drill 80. Repeated spikes by the same player. This teaches him to move back quickly so as to be ready to make another spike. The diagonal spike is the easiest spike to make, since in most cases it follows the angle of the run-up. There are certain variations on this basic spike: spiking whilst turning in the air, the windmill spike, spiking a ball that is rising (short spike), placed spikes and dummy spikes.

The 'turning spike' angles the ball away from the direction of the run-up. The player, already at the height of his jump, allows the ball to travel right across his body and then turns in the air to hit it in a direction opposed to his original run-up. To perform this spike well, the player must be closer to the ball than for the normal diagonal spike.

Drill 81. (i) Jumping on the spot and turning 45° in the air; (ii) same drill with a run-up, turning away from the angle of the run-up; (iii) same drill near the net.

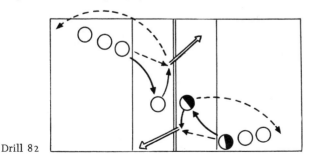

Drill 82

Drill 82. Player holds a tennis ball, hand ball or volleyball in his spiking hand. He runs up, jumps, turns in the air and, with a spike action, throws the ball across the net.

For this movement in the air to be effective, the player must trick the opposition block by running up and jumping as if for an ordinary spike. He only changes direction when already in the air. For the ball to be hit hard, the whole body must enforce the arm-action. This means that the ball must be hit having travelled beyond and across the player's body, at head height.

Drill 83. Practise turning spikes, from sets that are higher than usual.

Drill 84. Practise precision by spiking at pre-defined zones.

Drill 85. This drill is to teach players to look at the opposition block. Two players stand on a bench near to the net in the opposite court. One or other of these players lifts his arms, at the net, the moment that the spiker feeds the ball to the setter. The spiker either spikes them diagonally across the obstruction or turns in the air and spikes down the line. This drill should be repeated until the spiker can avoid the obstruction, even when the players only raise their hands as the setter passes the ball to the spiker.

The windmill spike is so called because of the rotational arm-movement. The run-up is more oblique than for other kinds of spike and, at the moment of take-off, the feet are almost parallel to the net. This affects the angle of the body and in particular of the shoulder and non-spiking arm.

The non-spiking arm and shoulder rise higher than in an ordinary spike. The spiking arm and shoulder, after swinging upwards to gain elevation, swing rapidly back down, behind and up in a circular movement. The trunk snaps forward at the moment of impact. For a windmill spike to be possible, the set must be further back from the net than for a normal spike. Drills 64, 65, 66, 68, 70, 74, 76, 77, 79, and 81 can be used to practise the windmill spike.

The windmill spike is rarely employed nowadays. Occasionally it is used to rectify a wrongly-judged approach or to deal with a ball that has been set too far from the net. It also has the advantage that the ball is hit later than with other types of spike and for this reason can often trick the block.

It is difficult to spike a rising ball and this shot should only be attempted by the best players, having a great deal of experience. Such a spike involves rapidly assessing the eventual flight of the ball by watching the way the setter moves. Contrary to the other types of spike, the movement involves running up and jumping at the same time, or even before, the ball leaves the setter's hands. By definition, the spiker must be in the air at the moment the ball is rising. Occasionally the spiker may be able to hit the ball precisely at the height of its flight.

The run-up should be reduced by one pace, to help the co-ordination of spiker and setter. As the whole action must be extremely fast, the spiker's arms swing forwards a fraction earlier. To help players to move faster, the sets can gradually be made lower and shorter and the spiker, starting with a normally-timed approach, gradually coming in earlier.

Drill 86. (i) The coach throws the ball to the setter. The spiker starts his run-up at the moment the ball leaves the coach's hands. (ii) As before, only the coach volleys the ball.

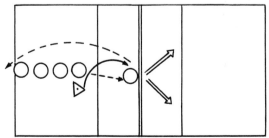

Drill 86

The coach must ensure, from the start, that players either spike diagonally in the direction of the run-up, or turn in the air and spike down the line (or diagonally to the other side of the block). If there is a block, a spiker should avoid spiking straight into it. It is extremely difficult to help a player to stop spiking into the block, once he has acquired the habit.

Much practice is required to perform the short spike correctly. It is a highly spectacular shot that is used by all the best teams. It has the great advantage of allowing the spiker to catch the opposition block and back-court defence unawares.

Some writers draw a distinction between dummy and normal spikes. This is unnecessary. To be of any use, the run-up, jump and trunk movement of the dummy spike must be identical to that of the ordinary spike: only the spiking action is different. The dummy may consist of a spike action changed into (i) a lob (no follow-through), (ii) a dump (the ball taken on the fingers of one hand), or (iii) a volley. The term 'dummy spike' is also used to describe the complete spike action that is made, usually by the No. 3 player, to disguise the fact that the ball is to be set to another player.

A dummy shot that is performed without the complete spike action is of little use, since it can easily be read by the opposition players. If the opposition are properly misled by the dummy action, they will form the defence required for a strong spike. This they will never do if they realise from the start that the strong spike is not forthcoming. They will easily move to the ball and receive it with a volley.

The dummy spike is especially effective when made from a good set. Where the spiker is under pressure, through a bad set or a mis-calculated run-up, the dummy rarely causes the opponents any difficulty.

9   The Block

The block is the first line of defence against a spike. It is formed close to and above the net and may be made above the opponents' court area. The block may be formed by one, two or three players.

To make a block the player must stand upright, his elbows close to his body, his arms bent and his hands held at shoulder-height. Sometimes the player will have to pause after moving into the right position but often the block is immediately preceded by a movement sideways. The jump is normally a standing jump, the power coming uniquely from the player's legs. Unlike the spike action, in the block there is rarely any arm-movement involved. The arms must be fully extended, without touching the net or obstructing any other player.

The wrists are locked, the fingers spread, tensed and slightly cupped (thumbs side by side) in an attempt to make as wide an obstruction as possible. The ball is attacked by a capping movement made by the hands, forearms and (by tall players with a high jump, who reach easily over the net), the shoulders as well.

To make a good block, the players must (i) stand close to the net; (ii) jump vertically; (iii) keep their shoulders

parallel to the net; (iv) correctly gauge the flight (height, speed and distance) of the ball; and (v) be able to adapt to the spiker's action.

Technically, a one-man block is quite easy to perform. However, its tactical application is very difficult. This is why the best blockers are always to be found amongst players who have had a long experience of the game. The one-man block is normally used by an inexperienced team or in certain specific situations, e.g. when blocking a spike that is hit on the second touch and at the beginning of a match against a team with a fast complex attack that is hard to read.

The block must first be practised without a ball.

Drill 87. The players stand in a line and perform the blocking action, jumping on the spot.

Drill 88. The players stand in a line, in pairs facing each other. The two partners of each pair should be roughly the same height. At the coach's signal, the players make a blocking action, trying to touch their partner's hands when at the highest point of their jump. The players must avoid bumping into or landing on each other.

Drill 89. Same as 87, but at the coach's signal the players first move forwards or sideways.

Drill 90. Players in pairs. One of each pair moves forwards or sideways, makes the blocking action, moves again and repeats. The other partner is facing and in front of him, jumping to block at the same time.

Drill 91. A line of players stand facing the wall, 40 or 50 centimetres from it. They practise blocking to different specific heights, as directed by the coach.

Drill 92. Same drill, but the jump is preceded by a step forward.

Drill 93. Players side-step in front of the wall, making a block after each step.

Drill 94. The same drill but stepping diagonally towards the wall, (see drill 98).

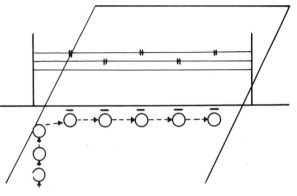

Drill 93

Drill 95. Players jump simultaneously and try to touch their partner's hands across the top of the net.

Drill 96. Still in pairs, on either side of net, but standing 1m 50 from the net. Together, the players step forward, block, step back, step forward, block, etc. This rhythm can be varied by making the players block two or three times, each time they come to the net.

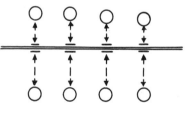

Drill 96

Drill 97. A line of players stands on either side of the net. In turn, the players block, side-step, block, the length of the net. The number of steps taken between blocks can be varied. It is important that after each side-step, or number of side-steps, the player regains balance and correct stance for jumping, before making the block.

Drill 98. Same drill, with diagonal approaches to the net.

From this point, drills with the ball can be introduced.

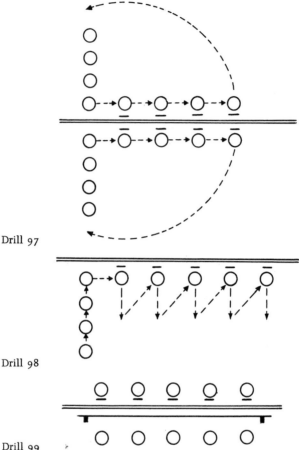

Drill 97

Drill 98

Drill 99

Drill 99. A line of players on one side of the net, standing on a bench and each holding a ball above the net. Their partners must jump and cap the ball with their hands. The height of the ball can be varied. After a number of repetitions, each player changes with his partner.

Drill 100. Same as above, but the player must move forwards before jumping.

Drill 101. Same again but the player moves sideways before jumping.

Drill 102. Same set up as drill 99. The players on the bench lob the ball downwards. Their partners have to choose the right moment to jump.

Drill 103. Same drill but the players on the bench tap the ball instead of lobbing it.

Drill 104. Same drill but the players move forwards, sideways or diagonally before blocking.

Drill 105. Same line-up. The players on the bench spike their balls into the blockers' hands. The blockers jump each time their partner lifts his arm to spike.

Drill 106. Same drill but the spiker volleys the ball once above his head before spiking. (i) The blocker stands at the net; (ii) the blocker moves forwards, sideways or diagonally into position, before blocking.

Drill 107. The coach, standing on a bench or a table, spikes the ball diagonally to one side or the other. The players stand in line on the other side of the net and block in turn. The coach warns the player which side he will

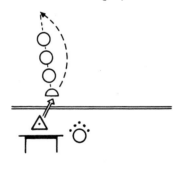

Drill 107

spike. The player must block by turning his outside hand towards the spiker's arm.

Drill 108. Same as 107 but the blocker must move sideways or obliquely to the blocking position.

Drill 109. As 107 and 108 but with the coach spiking down the line.

Drill 110. As 107–109 but with a player setting to the coach.

Drill 111. Same drills but with the coach varying the direction of his spikes without warning the blocker.

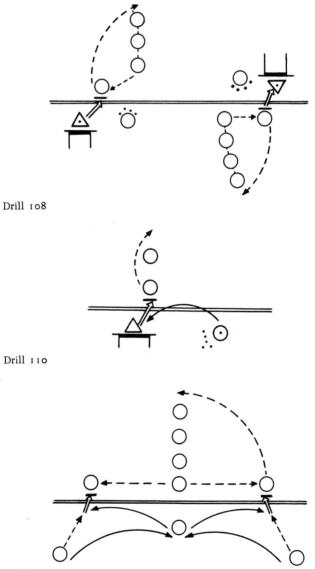

Drill 108

Drill 110

Drill 112

Drill 1 1 2. A player in position 3 sets to spikers in 4 and 2. On the other side of the net, the blocker in position 3 moves to block in positions 2 and 4. After two blocks the player goes to the back of the queue. The blockers are warned in which direction the balls will be spiked.

Drill 1 1 3. Same as 1 1 2, only the blockers are not told in which direction the ball will be spiked.

The two- or three-man block is much more effective, since it covers a greater angle of attack. Technically, it is very difficult, in that it requires a high level of co-ordination between the players involved. The difficulty is increased if the players are not the same height. The players do not necessarily have to jump at the same time: the essential factor is that their hands should be side by side at the moment the ball is to be blocked. This means that short players must jump earlier, since tall players need less time to reach the same height.

The position of the players in relation to the net is also important. If the players' hands are to form a single level obstruction, they must be positioned in the same plane. This means that, having moved together, the players should be shoulder to shoulder and parallel to the net, before jumping to block. Occasionally, this is not possible and the players then have to correct their position in the air, by moving their hands and arms. However, once the correct position, side by side and parallel to the net, has been reached the only other movement required is to turn the outside hand to face the direction of the spike. The other hands stay in the same plane.

The decision as to which player should lead the block depends partly on the standard of play. When the standard is low, the block must be led by the more experienced player. With a higher standard of play and when the players are equally experienced, it will depend on the attack. It will then be the player who is nearest to the point of the attack who leads the block. Since synchronisation of the

two- or three-man block is so difficult, a great many drills
without the ball are needed to teach and perfect it. These
drills are all very demanding and the number of repetitions,
the rhythm, the duration and period between each drill
should be carefully controlled.

Drill 114

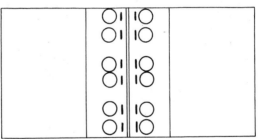

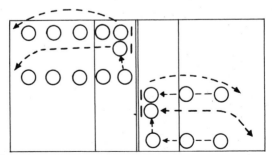

Drill 114. Players stand in pairs at the net and, at the coach's signal, form a synchronised block. Eventually, one of the players can give the signal.

Drill 115. On both sides of the net, two lines of players, one metre apart. One of the two players in front moves sideways beside the other and they jump forming a block.

Drill 116. The same line-up but the two lines stand 2 metres apart. Both players in front move sideways towards each other and jump, forming a block.

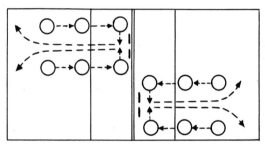

Drill 116

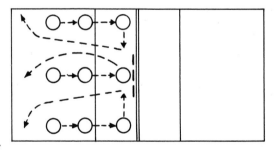

Drill 117

Drill 117. Three lines of players, so that the front players are respectively in positions 2, 3 and 4. Players in 2 and 4 move sideways beside 3. All three players jump to form a 3-man block. Player 3 waits for the other two players and then leads the block.

Drill 118. Same line-up. Player in position 3 moves alternately beside players in 4 and 2, and forms 2-man blocks. After several repetitions, the lines change.

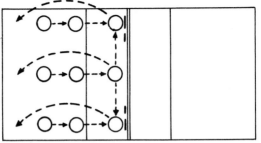

Drill 118

Drills 115 to 118 can be repeated, moving diagonally to the block position. The drill can be made more complicated as the players' movements become more synchronised. For example, with drill 115, the players can perform three blocks in succession. For the first, the player in the centre moves to the outside player; the second can be made from the same position; and for the third, the outside player can move back and run forwards to the block position.

Drill 119 involves using a ball. In court A, there are four

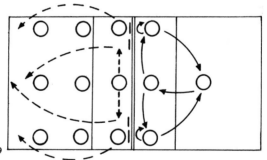

Drill 119

players, in positions 2, 3, 4 and 6. In court B, there are three lines of three players. In court A, player 6 volleys to No. 3. No. 3 volleys to 2 or 4, who catches the ball and throws it overhand into the other court. The player in the middle line watches to see which way the No. 3 passes the ball and then moves in that direction to block the throw, together with his outside man. The three blockers go to the end of the queue after having made a block at each end of the net. The object of the drill is to teach the players to synchronise their movements in relation to the ball and the opponent.

Later on, drill 107 can be used with a two-man instead of a one-man block. The coach should do the spiking. Drills 108 to 111 and 117 can follow, each with a two-man block. Finally drill 112 can be repeated with a two-man block and normal spikes.

10   Rolls and Dives

Back-rolls, side-rolls and dives can be grouped together. The difference between rolls and dives is that the rolls are made without the hands touching the ground whereas, when diving, the hands touch the ground first. These skills are used less than previously because (i) the dig has become so widely used, (ii) players are covering the ground faster and better, (iii) teams are using better systems of defence, and (iv) there is a new concern to economise effort so as to allow a more intelligent use of the other skills.

The dives and rolls are made from unbalanced positions. They are used whenever a player has not time to move into a balanced position to perform an ordinary volley or dig. In such cases the player falls as he performs the shot. Rolls and dives are ways of falling that allow the player to concentrate on playing a difficult ball without hurting himself. Obviously these shots are only played when the player is unable to play the ball from a balanced position. As he learns to read an attack more quickly and to move faster, the player has less need to dive and roll.

Dives and rolls are only used in extreme cases, when no other solution is possible. Physically they are more demanding than a rapid movement to a balanced position followed by a controlled volley or dig. Whilst diving or rolling, the player must have perfect control of his body. Initial drills are performed without a ball and are in fact elementary gymnastic exercises which allow the players to get used to hitting the floor.

When making a back-roll, the player starts in a basic stance but his centre of gravity swings backwards at the moment he plays the ball. His knees bend further, he rounds his back, and his behind sinks towards the ground, till he is sitting on his heels. The knee of his back leg is near to his chest, whilst his front leg is stretched out in front of him. The ball is played at a level with his chin. His arms and wrists propel the ball as his upper body falls backwards from an angle of about 45°.

Drill 120. Players are in pairs facing each other. One player adopts a basic stance and gradually slips down until sitting on his heels. His partner helps to break his fall as he rounds his back and rolls over. This movement is repeated, the partner giving less and less help as the player's confidence increases. The player should roll forwards again on to his feet, without using his hands, using his extended front foot to swing him forwards.

Drill 121. The players start in a line, move forwards, check, and then do a back roll. Slow at first, the drill can gradually be speeded up.

Drill 122. The floor is marked out with a number of lines. The players move around in the basic stance position and make a back-roll whenever they cross one of the lines.

Drills 121 and 122 can be performed with the players holding a ball in their hands. This prevents them from using their hands to get back on their feet. At this point drills with the ball can be introduced.

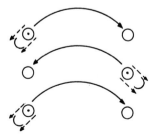

Drill 123

Drill 123. Players stand in pairs, in two lines, 5 to 7 metres apart. One partner feeds, the other runs forwards, crouches and returns the ball with a back-roll volley. This drill can also be done alone, by throwing the ball against a wall.

Drill 124. Two lines of players stand 3 to 5 metres apart. The players in one line throw a fairly high ball to their partners who, from a low position, dive to return the ball. As the drill is repeated, the feeder gives increasingly difficult balls.

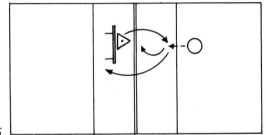

Drill 125

Drill 125. The coach stands on a table, near to the net and feeds the ball to a player in the opposite court. The player must make a back-roll, volleying the ball to a particular point (e.g. near to the net, across the net to the coach, etc.)

Drill 126. Two lines of players both stand facing the wall. The back line throws the balls at the wall and their partners return the ball by volleying it back against the wall, whilst making a back-roll. The drill should not be conducted too slowly.

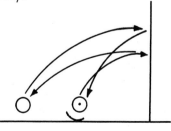

Drill 127

Drill 127. Players stand in pairs, 6 to 11 metres apart. One player serves softly at the other who volley returns the ball with a back-roll.

Drill 128. The same drill with the feeder giving soft spikes.

Drill 129. The same as 128 only over the net.

The *side-roll* differs from the back-roll in that it is preceded by a movement to the side. The player, from a crouch position, sinks on to one heel as he turns to face the direction

in which he wants to volley. He rolls on to his back in the same way as when doing a back-roll. In volleying, as he falls and turns, the pressure of his outside arm is greater than that of the other. The drills for practising the back-roll can be modified for practising the side-roll. Instead of moving forwards before rolling the player moves sideways.

Drill 130. The coach, in position 3, feeds a line of players by throwing the balls into zone 2 or 4. The players move under the ball and volley it back by means of a side-roll.

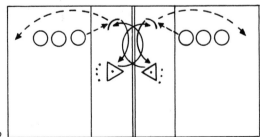

Drill 130

Drill 131. A player in position 2 feeds balls the width of the court to the 3-metre line. The first player of a line in position 6 moves to making a precise side-roll volley return to the feeder. On the other side of the net, the feeder can feed balls from position 4 to position 2.

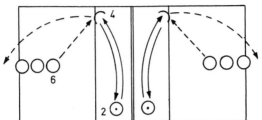

Drill 131

A variation of the side-roll volley is the side-roll dig. The movement is identical but the ball is played on the wrist or clenched fist of one fully extended arm. This variation allows little control but is used to save a ball that is falling so far to one side that it is impossible to volley.

The dive forwards is difficult to learn. Before teaching the skill, the coach must ensure that the players all have enough strength in their arms to perform the skill without danger. The dive can be introduced with some preliminary strengthening and gymnastic exercises.

Exercise 132. From the press-up position, the player throws one leg backwards into the air.

Exercise 133. From a crouch position, the player falls forwards on to his hands, slowly lowering his chest to the ground. The exercise should be repeated, increasing the initial distance from the ground.

Exercise 134. From a crouch position, the player springs forwards, landing on his hands, one leg remaining on the ground, his arms lowering the body to the ground (first the chest, then the stomach, and finally the thighs).

Exercise 135. Same as 134, preceded by a short run-up.

Exercise 136. Without a run-up, the player dives both feet leaving the ground.

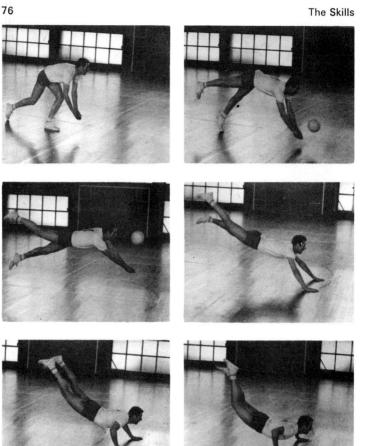

Exercise 137. As 136, preceded by a run-up.

As the dive improves, the player must add the action of hitting the ball with the back of his hand, before touching the ground.

Eventually, he will be able to hit the ball with either hand.

When first using the balls, the feeder should throw them close enough for the player to dive and retrieve them from a standing position. Later the distance can be increased, so that the player has to sprint forwards, before diving to play the ball.

Some authors consider separately the action of recovering a ball from the net. Although the circumstances are different, the action required is always some kind of volley, dig, dive or roll. A ball coming from the net is often difficult to play because of its speed and low flight, which force the player to roll or dive. To take the ball well, the player must note (i) where the ball goes into the net, (the lower it hits the net, the further it will rebound), and (ii) at what angle the ball goes into the net, (it will come out at the same angle).

How far the player succeeds in his recovery depends largely on how fast he moves into position. The ball should be played at the point in its flight that is furthest from the net and still playable. The object is to extract the ball from the danger area near the net. The method of playing the ball will depend on the way in which the ball went into the net, on the distance the player is from the ball and on his physical and technical abilities. The ideal shot is one that allows an immediate counter-attack. According to the situation, the player will use either a volley, a dig, a roll or a dive.

Chapter Two : Tactics and Systems of Play

1   General Observations

One of the best definitions of tactics is that made by Professors Theodorescu and Predescu in their book *The Problems of Training in Team Games*. 'Tactics are the totality of the individual and collective actions of a team, organised and co-ordinated rationally within the limits of the rules and of sportsmanship, with the object of success—the qualities and peculiarities of the players of the team being considered together with the weaknesses of their opponents.'

Systems, whether of attack or defence, are of little use unless they are chosen to suit the technical and physical abilities of the players concerned. By the same token, there is rarely any point in copying the systems employed by a particular team of great experience (tactics which that team employs most successfully) : these systems will not correspond with the technical ability of a team of a lower standard.

One often sees teams that have adopted the latest ideas of the big international teams. For example, the penetration system of attack, where a player from the back line comes forward to set, is often used nowadays. This system of attack, which is profitable for a team with three players at the net, all able to spike well, is of no use to a team that has only one real spiker. Then, all that the other two front-line players can do is watch. The opposition will quickly realise that the number of attackers is no greater and will put all its blocking power on to the one good spiker. On the other hand, the risk of bad sets is always greater when the setter is a back-line player than when the setter is in the front line. Worse still, there are women's teams, without a single real spiker, which adopt penetration because it is fashionable and used by the big teams.

Recently there was a French first division team that tried to imitate the East Germans. They used a four-man reception of service and placed their two setters close to the net, with the idea of producing a greater variety of attack. Unfortunately their reception of service was too weak to allow them to use the system effectively. Their setters were forced to run back to the back court to recover balls which were going far from their intended zone. Sometimes they were unable to reach the ball at all. The coach was wrong to choose a system that was not geared to the technical standard and physical ability of his players.

The actions of the players are determined by the rules and object of the game. A team attempts to gain the number of points necessary to win a set and ultimately the match. The points are won by playing the ball, according to the rules, in a way that either makes it impossible for the opponents to return the ball or else forces them to make mistakes.

Since the rules require that the players rotate, they should be all-round players, equally good as spikers, back-court players, blockers, setters and servers. The more versatile the players, the easier it is to form a team. However, there are very few teams which correspond to the ideal: rarely are all the players equally good at all the component roles of the game. There are always some players who are better at spiking than defending. Tall players tend to be less good at setting; short players are usually good in defence and at setting but, due to their lack of height, make poor spikers.

This means that, in the end, the coach is forced to use

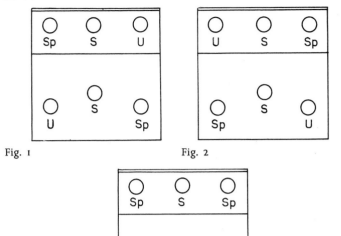

Fig. 1   Fig. 2

Fig. 3

players in special roles—principally as spikers, universals or setters. When composing a team for a match, the coach takes their specialist abilities into account. One of the most widespread of all line-ups, which is equally good in attack and defence, consists of two spikers, two universals and two setters. The line-up (from positions 1 to 6) is spiker, universal, setter, spiker, universal, setter (Fig. 1).

A second possible line-up, with the same players, is shown in Fig. 2. Fig. 3 shows a line-up that involves three spikers and three setters. This line-up strengthens the defence yet still presents a satisfactory attack.

There is also the five spikers/one setter line-up. This permits a stronger attack which is, however, more difficult to organise. It is particularly difficult when the setter is in Position 5. There are still other possible line-ups. For example, a line-up that is commonly used by beginners, consists of two spikers and four setters.

At present, the most effective of these is the two spikers/

two universals/two setters. This permits a varied attack and yet assures mobility and greater effectiveness in defence. If the coach can improve his spikers' volley and back-court play, and his setters' block and spike, he will be approaching the ideal team of six all-round players. The team is then bound to be effective throughout, whilst continuing to benefit from the special abilities of the individual players. It is no longer possible today to play top-level volleyball with a team of narrowly specialised players.

2   Individual Tactics

Since the game is composed of a succession of individual and group actions, there are individual as well as group tactics. An individual makes tactical use of his technical skills, to help the team as a whole. The more he is able to enlarge his performance of each of the skills, the greater his choice in dealing with each situation within the game.

Learning the technical possibilities of the various skills is closely tied to learning the skills themselves. Once a skill has been learnt through a number of simple drills, the player must develop his control and use of the skills through more complex drills that are nearer to the game situation. For example, in a game, a spiker has several problems to solve at the moment he has to hit the ball: he must gauge the flight of the ball, bypass the opposition block, and find a hole in the back-court defence. His value as a spiker depends on how he solves all these problems. He may decide, for instance, to spike diagonally inside the block, to spike down the line, to spike through the block if the block lacks cohesion, to spike out off the block, or to dump the ball over the block so that it lands in an undefended part of the attack zone. He has, in fact, a wide choice but very little time in which to make it, if his choice is to be effective.

The player will only possess this wide view of the game, have acquired the ability to adapt quickly to specific situations, and choose the right variant of the skill that he has to perform, if he has already been well prepared by repeatedly practising the whole range of actions that are possible when spiking.

In the same way, the player must know the many possible variations in the performance of each of the other skills, and the related tactical advantages of those variations. The drills for learning and practising each skill must be organised into a progression that teaches the player to think. They must teach him to choose quickly the variant of a given skill that will allow him best to solve each of the game situations in which he has to play the ball.

3 Group Tactics

3·1 General

Group tactics determine the common actions of a group of players who are attempting to recover the ball in defence and return it into the opposing court, in such a way that it cannot be recovered by the opposition. In volleyball, group tactics involve: (i) systems of attack, (ii) systems of defence and (iii) systems of service reception. In addition there are the tactics of serving. Although such classification is somewhat unconventional, it simplifies the task of teaching the tactics of volleyball.

In most team sports, the team will attack as soon as they gain possession of the ball. For the rest of the time, whilst the opponents have the ball, the team remains on the defensive. Although this is generally true of volleyball, there are certain complex situations which involve some players preparing to defend whilst their team still has possession of the ball. For example, players in certain positions relative to the spiker, should cover his attack in case he is blocked. Another such situation occurs when a team is serving: although the service is an attack, the rest of the players are already organised into a system of defence, in case the ball should be returned. Conversely, when the opponents have the ball, players at the net often prepare a counter attack: a strong team will put up an attacking block.

This said, the main characteristic of volleyball is a continuous rapid change from one situation to another, before a particular action of attack or defence is fully completed. This complicates the players' role and, at all levels of play, frequently causes moments of confusion.

At any given moment, all six players in a volleyball team are actively playing a role, even though the formation of a attack only involves three players touching the ball. For example, on service reception, the player in zone 5 might receive the ball, dig it to the player in zone 3, who might in turn volley it to the spiker in zone 4. Although only three players touch the ball, this sequence of play involves a co-ordinated activity of the entire team. The players in the other zones (6, 1 and 2) are covering throughout: first they cover players 5 and 3, in case they fail to control the ball properly and then they cover player 4, in case he is blocked. All too often, players are not prepared for such contingencies and are content to stand and watch, believing they will not be required to play the ball. This is a very big mistake and one that severely limits the team's performance.

3·2   Systems of Attack

Systems of attack, whether simple or complex, involve two, three or four players at the net and are designed to penetrate the opponents' defence. These systems are established before the beginning of the game, according to the abilities of the players in the team, and the different situations which can arise during the game. Their application depends on how difficult it is to recover the ball after the opponents' attack and the distribution of spiking power on the team's own side of the net. The players must also consider how best to profit from the weaknesses of the opposition. The players must know which opposition players have a poor volley or dig, which are often out of position, which blockers are short or have a low jump, etc. A team must always try to impose its own tactics on the opposition and disallow them the initiative.

The systems are therefore applied freely and creatively by the players, who must choose the best available solution for each situation, as it occurs. The solutions do not depend entirely on the inspiration of the individual player, since the choice and element of invention must always be based on the systems that were pre-arranged. The player is limited to a choice based on the systems that were thought out and practised previously at the team training sessions.

Several systems of attack are possible and they depend on various elements, e.g. (i) whether the ball is played twice or three times, (ii) the number of players involved—i.e. the front-line players only, or a player from the back-line as well, (iii) whether players switch positions, (iv) whether several players run in to spike at the same time, etc. There follows a study of these different possibilities, beginning with the most simple systems, those that can be adopted by teams of any standard.

Figures 4 to 7 show examples of a basic medium-length set. The ball is set by a front-line player to the player next to him in the line-up.

Figure 8 shows similar sets but the pass to the setter is longer.

Fig. 4   Fig. 5

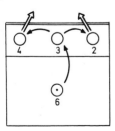
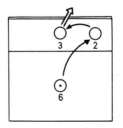

Fig. 6   Fig. 7

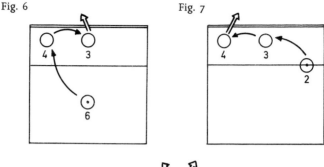

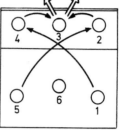

Fig. 8

By contrast, an attack can be built with a long or cross-court set, from one side of the court to the other (normally from No. 2 to No. 4 or vice versa) (Fig. 9). Any team must be able to use at least these two systems of attack.

The players in the attacking team who do not actually touch the ball must be clear about their supporting role. In any system of attack, the formation of the other team's defence must be considered, especially their defence at the net. This defence is designed to prevent the ball crossing into

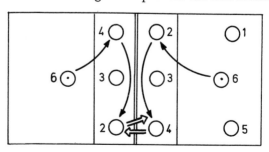

Fig. 9

their court and to redirect it as quickly as possible into the court of the attacking team. The players not directly involved in the attack must take care of this possible counter-attack, and prevent the ball touching the ground in their own court, should their spiker be well blocked. In fact all five players support the spiker by 'covering the spike'. Between them, they are responsible for defending the entire court against a possible attacking block.

There are two common systems of covering the spiker.

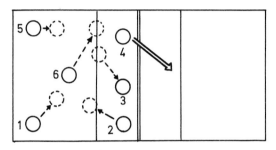

Fig. 10

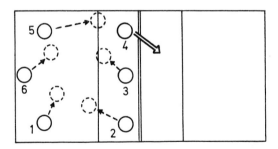

Fig. 11

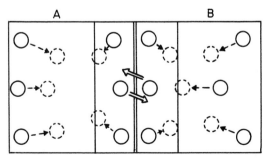

Fig. 12

In the first, player no. 6 moves forwards, and in the second he stays back. Figs. 10 and 11 show these two systems when the spike is made from position 4.

Fig. 12 shows the two systems when the spike is from the centre of the net. The team in Court A have No. 6 back. In court B the No. 6 covers close to the spiker.

The following tactical moves and systems of attack are for teams which already have some experience.

Switches are used (i) to improve the conditions for attack—these switches being made before the attack is

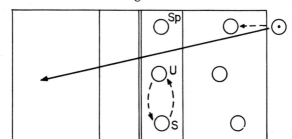

Fig. 13

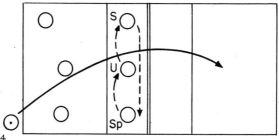

Fig. 14

staged; and (ii) to surprise the opposition—these switches being made at the last moment, as the attack is being built.

Figs 13 and 14 show players switching as their own server hits the ball. This is the simplest switching tactic. More difficult, however, is the switch that is made whilst the opposition serve. The players must move very much faster yet still be able to receive service correctly.

The most effective and difficult switches are those made by the attacking team at the moment the setter plays the ball. In Fig. 16, as No. 2 passes to zone 4, No. 4 switches to zone 3 and No. 3 moves into zone 4 and spikes. In Fig. 17, No. 2 makes an overhead set and No. 3 runs behind him to spike.

When the two front-line players run in simultaneously to spike, one receives the ball and the other performs a dummy action. The move will be successful if the actions of both

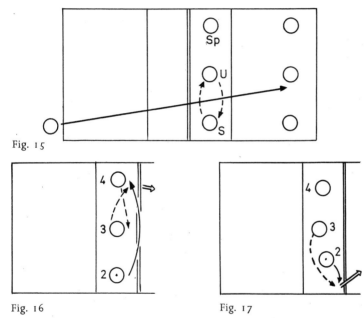

Fig. 15

Fig. 16   Fig. 17

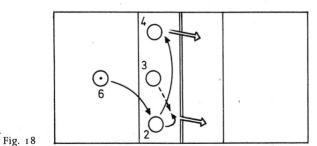

Fig. 18

players are correct and synchronised with the setter's movements.

In Fig. 18, No. 6 passes the ball to No. 2, who can either make a short pass to No. 3 or a low cross-court pass to No. 4. Whichever set is made, players 3 and 4 must both make the complete run-up and spike actions if the dummy-action attack is to be introduced and the opposition caught on the wrong foot. As shown in the diagram, No. 3 runs close to the setter, starting his run before the ball leaves the setter's hands and being prepared to hit the ball whilst it is still rising. Almost immediately, No. 4 runs up and jumps at the far end of the net.

The *penetration system of attack* is considerably more complicated. The number of potential spikers is raised to three by one of the back-court players moving to the net to play the role of setter.

This system is much more difficult because of the great strain that is put on the penetrating setter. He has to play a number of roles in quick succession, set from many positions, and still be able to set precisely. Usually the penetrating setter is either No. 1 or No. 6, depending on which of the two can set best.

The main advantage of penetration is that the opposition must be prepared to block in a greater number of positions along the net. Fig. 19 shows penetration by players 1 and 6, and the three possible sets they can make. However, to make penetration even more effective, dummy-action spikes and

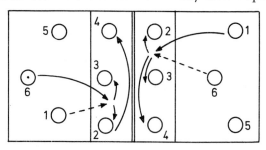

Fig. 19

switching can also be introduced into the attack. This requires the synchronisation of the movements of all four players taking part and extra precision in the setting.

In Fig. 20, No. 6 penetrates and makes a normal medium-height set. No. 3 runs in and jumps close to No. 6, as he sets, and makes a dummy-action spike, whilst No. 2 switches by running behind No. 3 jumps a split second later, and spikes the ball. Meantime, No. 6 can still decide to set either a high or a low long ball to No. 4.

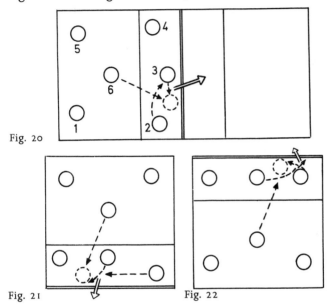

Fig. 20

Fig. 21

Fig. 22

Fig. 21 shows another variation, in which No. 6 penetrates and makes the same set. No. 3 runs in as before and No. 4 runs in to spike where No. 2 spiked previously. This time No. 6 has the further possibility of setting overhead to No. 2.

In Fig. 22, No. 6 penetrates and makes a normal overhead set. No. 2 runs in for a short overhead set and No. 3 runs behind No. 2, jumping a fraction later, and spikes. No. 6 could also set to No. 4.

In all three examples, the player who runs in for the short set could spike himself (i.e. No. 3 in Figs. 20 and 21, and No. 2 in Fig. 22). The penetration system, then, allows a whole range of variation in attack which, if properly performed, would make it impossible for the opposition to put up an effective block at the right moment. This combination of penetration, dummy-action spikes and switching is now used by all good teams because (i) service and opposition spikes are now universally received with a dig, which, being less accurate than a volley, is less likely to suggest that a front-line player might spike on the second touch; and (ii) under these circumstances, some other means of counteracting the block, which otherwise is far too strong, has to be found.

A team able to use these complex systems of attack is stronger. It also provides a variety that is the essence of a truly spectacular game.

The *spike on the second touch*, or the dummy spike that is converted at the last minute into a set was very popular until a short time ago. Now it is less used for the reasons mentioned above.

The value of this shot is evident. If the first ball is passed precisely to a position near the net from which it can be spiked, a spiker running up and jumping to hit the ball will either have only a one-man block to contend with or else will draw the opposition into a two-man block so that his jump-set to another spiker allows that spiker an opening. The set must, however, be fast and low, so as to prevent the blockers from recovering and moving to block a second time.

I personally feel that teams have abandoned this element of attack too soon. Penetration is now used throughout the the game, even when a good first pass would allow a second-touch spike or dummy-action spike to be made. Even at the highest level of the game there are often times when the opposition is forced to return a high soft ball that is easily controlled. Usually when this happens a back-court player penetrates, another player digs the easy ball to him and the three spikers run in to spike.

In my opinion, this is quite wrong. On such occasions, a team should always spike on the second touch—or set in the air, if the spike action draws a two-man block. A second touch spike not only puts pressure on the opposition blockers but in most cases will also catch the back-court defenders unprepared.

However, there are perhaps other technical reasons for teams not using this tactic of attack. The first pass must be precise, and preferably from a fairly acute angle. The spiker (normally No. 2, sometimes No. 4, rarely No. 3) should be facing the ball. The pass should not be too hard and neither too near or too far from the net, so that the spiker can either spike or turn and set in the air. The spiker must be used to spiking from such passes, otherwise he will not catch his opponents wrongfooted and will allow them to take the initiative. If he then decides to set, he will set without managing to draw the block and, moreover, his set will be bad. This will leave the third player in the worst possible position, having to spike a badly placed ball through a well-formed block. These are big risks for players who are not highly skilled and pushes them towards less demanding tactics on which to base their attack.

Recommended first-touch sets are No. 6 to Nos. 4 or 2;

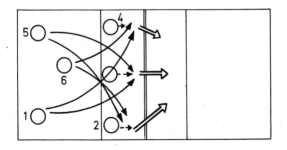

Fig. 23

No. 5 to No. 2 or No. 3 (especially if he is left-handed); and
No. 1 to Nos. 3 or 4 (see Fig. 23).

Front-line players may also make first-touch sets (see
Fig. 24): No. 2 to Nos. 3 or 4; No. 3 to Nos. 2 or 4; and
No. 4 to Nos. 3 or 2.

First-touch sets may be combined with all the other
systems and tactics of attack already mentioned—with
short or long, normal or fast sets, with dummy spikes and
with switching. Fig. 25 shows an example. The No. 1

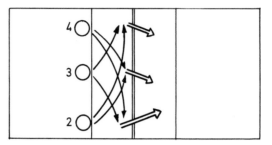

Fig. 24

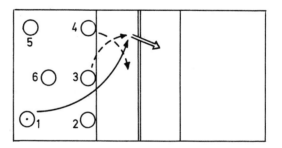

Fig. 25

passes straight to the net, to a point between Nos. 3 and 4.
No. 4 does a dummy-action spike and sets overhead, close
to him. No. 3 runs behind him and spikes. No. 4 could also
spike himself or give either a normal or a fast set to No. 2.

Fig. 26 shows another possible combination. No. 6 sets
the first ball directly to No. 3. No. 3—and immediately
after him Nos. 4 and 2—runs in to spike at the centre of the
net. No. 3 can either spike himself or, in the air, set a short
set slightly forwards to No. 2 or slightly overhead to No. 4.

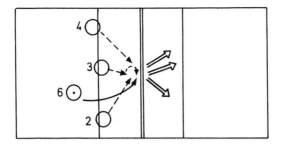

Fig. 26

Both Nos. 2 and 4 are able to spike the short set, since they are both already in the air.

All systems of attack used by experienced teams are an attempt to beat the defence in the following ways: (i) by increasing the number of players at the net; (ii) by making the attack so fast that the opposition no longer have time to form a proper block; (iii) by making dummy-action spikes so that the opposition do not know where to form the block; and (iv) by attacking along the whole length of the net, so that the blockers have the maximum amount of ground to cover.

The following progression of drills is recommended for teaching and improving each of the various tactical elements of the attack. (i) Begin by passing the ball and making the movements, without spiking the ball across the net. (ii) As before but add the spike across the net and a back-court defence on the other side. (iii) Begin the system by a simple service from the opposition court and add an opposition block to the set-up. (iv) Continue with increasingly difficult services and a complete opposition defence. (v) Introduce the system in a controlled game, in which the players have specific tasks to perform. Play without regular rotation to ensure a sufficient number of repetitions. (vi) Introduce the system in a match against a weaker team, so that the experience required for its introduction in a big match is gradually acquired.

From this point on, it is a matter of the players having to

learn when to introduce a particular system of attack, to appreciate the moment at which a given tactic would succeed. It must be realised that there are times during the game when a team should not attempt any complicated moves. Players learn to perform the difficult systems very well at training sessions but rarely manage them during a match. This is an ability that is acquired with difficulty and only with a great deal of training and experience.

3·3   Systems of Defence

Volleyball differs from other team games in that the players are not able to intervene to prevent the opposition forming an attack. Intervention can only be made at the precise moment that the attack is made. In fact, there is no move that is totally defensive. Apart from the block, any move to prevent the opposition from scoring constitutes the first phase of building an attack.

The team's movement into a defensive position both at the net and in the back court, at the completion of their attack, is made whilst the opposition constructs its own attack. Were it not for the fact that the opposition required time to construct an attack, the first team would be unable to move back and form a defence. Generally speaking, a player's movement in defence is determined by a chosen defensive system. However, within this structure it is vital that the player anticipates the direction and strength of the opposition's spike, otherwise he will only rarely be able to reach the ball. A normal spike propels the ball considerably faster than any defender can hope to move. This means that the chosen system of defence can only be a point of departure.

Each player must continually modify his position within the zone which is his to defend. Such modification is made according to the apparent intentions of the opposition. Surprising though it may be, despite its relatively small size, an entire volleyball court is too large for three or four players to defend, whilst the other two or three are blocking at the net. Defence can only be achieved according to certain principles.

The back-court defensive line-up depends on the position of the block. Once the zone defended by the block is established, the other players are positioned so that they can cover the rest of the court with the best chances of success. Finally, it must be decided how to cover behind the block. The defence is then structured.

There have long been two alternative systems of defence: the 3–2–1 (with No. 6 back) and the 3–1–2 (with No. 6 up). Recently the majority of teams have adopted the 3–2–1 system. This system has several variations and fits the requirements of a defensive system more appropriately. Fig. 27 shows this system. The shaded zone is covered by the block. No. 5 stands outside this zone, covering a spike made down the line. No. 1 positioned on the other side of the zone covers the diagonal. The No. 6, in the centre of the zone itself, is responsible for taking all the balls coming off the block into the zone and any soft spikes made over the block.

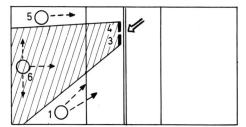

Fig. 27

The diagram doesn't show player No. 2. This is because he can be placed differently and play a different role, according to variations of the basic system. In Fig. 28, a first possibility, No. 2 retreats to the 3-metre line and is responsible for an oblique diagonal spike. The cover of the block is then made by the No. 5 who must come forward and pick up any ball that is falling directly behind the

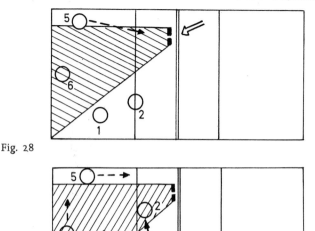

Fig. 28

Fig. 29

block. Practice has shown that this variant has two defects. Players No. 1 and 2 often get in each other's way—it being difficult to judge the flight of a ball that has been spiked hard—and the No. 5 player often hesitates and comes in too late to cover the block.

To counteract these defects another variation was introduced, which has since become widely used. This is to make the front-line player, who is not involved in the block, responsible for covering the block (see Fig. 29). This means that the immediate cover is always made by either No. 2 or No. 4 and that Nos. 5, 6 and 1 are not required to come up so far.

More recently a third variation has been introduced, resulting from the relatively new rule that permits the blockers to hit the ball a second time after blocking. In this variant the blockers (in Fig. 30, Nos. 3 and 4) are themselves responsible for the immediate cover and the No. 2 retreats behind the 3-metre line. The No. 6 man moves one pace to his left and there is then a four-man defence, set in roughly two semi-circles. When the ball goes just behind the reach of the blockers, it is the responsibility of either the No. 2 or the No. 5.

There exists one other variant of the 3–2–1 defence which is less used because of the great powers of anticipation and great speed of movement that it requires from the back-line players. Nevertheless, the variant is considered by certain specialists to be amongst the most advanced. It has

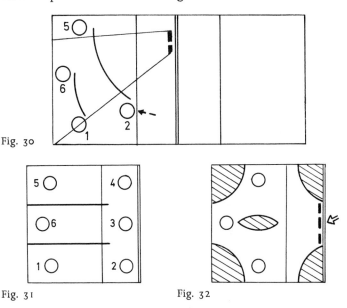

Fig. 30

Fig. 31

Fig. 32

been used several times by the Japanese women's national team and less often by the Russians. The court is divided lengthways into three zones and the Nos. 1, 6 and 5 must each defend a third of the court in front of them.

With each variant of the 3–2–1 system (except the last mentioned) the weak point is the centre of the court. When the cover of the block is made by Nos. 5 or 1, it is the position behind this player and the centre of the court which are vulnerable. The same applies when the front-line player not involved in the block is responsible for the cover.

When a three-man block is formed, the danger is greater still. In Fig. 32, all the shaded zones are vulnerable. If the three-man block succeeds in preventing a hard spike, the spiker still has far too many undefended zones that can be reached with a dump or a placed 'lobbed' spike. For this reason, a three-man block is only used against a powerful spiker, spiking in position 3, who is not used to dumping or 'lobbing' his spikes. When the player who is spiking from the centre of the net is an experienced player, the defence should only use a two-man block and place the other four players in the two semi-circle positions.

The 3–1–2 (No. 6 up) system of attack used to be the most popular. The line-up is simpler and players in the back line are not required to move so far forward. The No. 6 is responsible for covering the block and has no other function. In effect, the whole back court is defended by only two players, which means that they have far more ground to cover. Furthermore, these two players are placed in a zone that is already covered by the block (see Fig. 34). The zone left by the No. 6, in order to cover the block, is always very vulnerable. The system can be recommended, generally speaking, for beginners or for a team that has a bad block.

It is possible to adjust the defensive line-up, in certain rotational positions, in order to protect a weak back-court

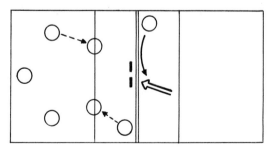

Fig. 33

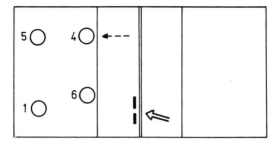

Fig. 34

player. In the 3–1–2 system the weak player can switch from position 1 and 5 into the No. 6 position, which is less demanding. In the 3–2–1 system, the weak player is switched into No. 6, at the back of the court, where the balls arrive less strongly.

Recently there has been a move towards specialisation in defence. By switching in the back court, players can occupy the same position every time they are in the back line. This improves the performance of a team in that it allows the best defender to be permanently in the most difficult position. First introduced by the East Germans, back-court switches are now being increasingly used at club level.

3·4 Tactics on Service
Service has become a weapon of attack and its tactical use is important. Generally speaking its object is not to score points directly but to make it more difficult for the opposition to organise an effective attack.

Only the team with service is able to score points. This team tries to retain service and scores points for as long as it does so. On losing service, a team must make every possible effort to regain it.

The brief moment before service is used by each team to organise its line-up. There follows an account of serving tactics and systems of service reception.

Given the importance of retaining service, the player who serves without thinking and makes a real gift to his

opponents must be condemned. Although service constitutes an attack, the other five players in the serving team
prepare to defend. The success of this defence will largely
depend on the service. If the service succeeds in putting
pressure on the opposition, it is likely that they will make an
easy return, which then allows the serving team to build an
effective counter-attack.

The server must adopt certain principles: (i) Aim for
consistency and precision rather than use any type of
service whose only advantage is strength. Generally
speaking, the more powerful the service, the less it is
precise and the more likely to make a fault. (ii) Always aim
at the weak point in the opposition's line-up, or at the
players whose reception is the least good. (iii) Seek out the
tension that is often felt by players receiving service:
continue to serve at a player who has already made a
mistake, serve at a player who has been substituted on
court and has not yet touched the ball. (iv) Use any
exterior factors which might help—the lighting or draughts
indoors, the sun or the wind out-of-doors. (v) As soon as he
has served, the server must move quickly to his position in
the defensive line-up.

As the player serves, his team form their defensive line-up
and make any switches necessary for the counter-attack.
Fig. 35 gives two examples of switching to strengthen the
defence. In court A, No. 1 switches with No. 6 as soon as he
has served. At the same time, No. 2, the best blocker in the

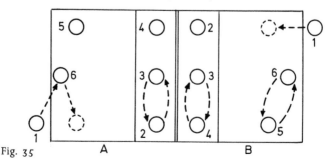

Fig. 35   A   B

front line, switches with No. 3 so that there will be a higher block in the centre. On court B, the same switches are made between Nos. 6 and 5 in the back line, and Nos. 4 and 3 at the net.

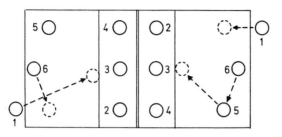

Fig. 36

Fig. 36 shows two examples of switching on service, with a 3–1–2 attack. In court A, after service, No. 1 moves quickly to the 3-metre line to cover the block and No. 6 takes the No. 1 defensive position. In court B, a similar switch is made between Nos. 6 and 5.

Fig. 37 shows a back-court switch in defence involving all three players. After No. 1 has served he moves to position

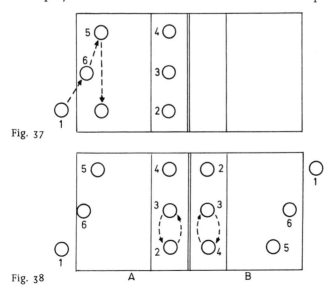

Fig. 37

Fig. 38

A   B

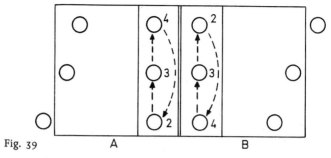

Fig. 39   A   B

No. 6, No. 6 moves to position No. 5 and No. 5 moves to position No. 1.

Fig. 38 shows switches whilst serving, to prepare a counter-attack. In court A, No. 3 switches with No. 2; in court B, No. 4 switches with No. 3.

Fig. 39 shows switches involving all three players in the front line, again to prepare a counter-attack. In court A, No. 4 (the setter) moves to position 2, No. 2 to position 3 and No. 3 to position 4. In court B, No. 4 (the setter), moves to position 3, No. 3 to position 2 and No. 2 to position 4.

Although a team adopts a defensive line-up to receive service, at the same time it must prepare to attack. The choice of system and the attack itself will depend on the accuracy of the dig with which the service is received. If the dig is made incorrectly, the rally stops and the team loses a point. If the dig is not a fault but lacks precision, the team will have little choice and will have difficulty in building an attack. The serving team will then have no difficulty in defence.

A good reception depends on certain principles, governing the individual player's technique and the line-up of the team as a whole. These depend on the quality of the opponent's service and the chosen system of attack. (i) On receiving service, each player must have a clearly defined zone to defend. He must make sure he can see the server's action and the flight of the ball (Fig. 40). (ii) On

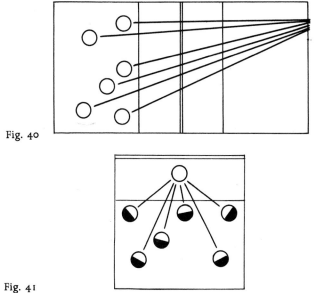

Fig. 40

Fig. 41

receiving service, the players must first be square to the server and then to the direction in which they intend to dig the ball (Fig. 41). (iii) Generally speaking, the line-up of the team must cover the most vulnerable zone (see Fig. 42). However, the line-up should expand or contract, depending on the type of service employed by the opposition.

Fig. 43 shows a contracted line-up to receive a powerful service. Fig. 44 two expanded line-ups, used to receive services that are relatively soft. N.B. Any line-up for service reception must allow players to move slightly forwards as

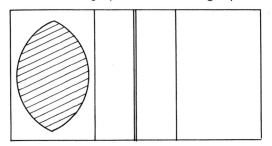

Fig. 42

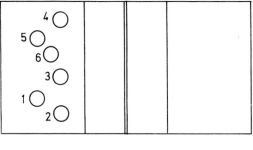

Fig. 43

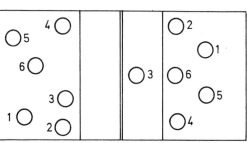

Fig. 44

they play the ball. As far as possible, players should avoid having to move backwards.

Fig. 45 shows two formations which are allied to systems of attack. In each case, the setter (in one case No. 3 in the other No. 2) is placed at the net and is exempted from receiving service. These two systems are appropriate for beginners and for teams with a little experience.

Fig. 46 illustrates another 5-man reception line-up. No. 6 in court A, and No. 1 in court B are setters and penetrate to

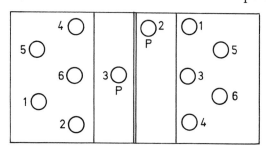

Fig. 45

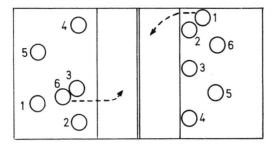

Fig. 46

the net on service. They are protected by players No. 3 and No. 2 respectively and do not take part in the reception.

Fig. 47 shows another 5-man reception line-up. The setter is No. 4 and is not involved in the reception. As the ball is served, he moves quickly into the No. 3 position. This system can be used by players not having a great deal of experience. At the moment the server hits the ball, the

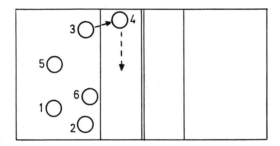

Fig. 47

No. 3 player must be slightly in front of No. 6 and to the right of No. 4.

It is clear that most systems of receiving service involve only five players. The systems have evolved comparatively recently but are now used by all good teams. It is, in fact, simpler for five players to receive service than six, since it helps to avoid any muddle. In any case, when the sixth player is not required to receive service, he is better able to fulfil the vital role of constructing the attack (i.e. deciding where to set and setting). Occasionally, a player who is particularly bad at receiving or a player who is hurt will be

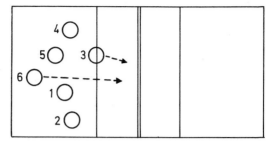

Fig. 48

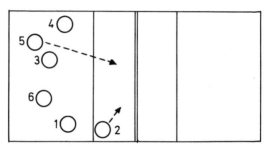

Fig. 49

placed in the sixth, non-involved position, so as to avoid
the risk of his losing points.

The East Germans introduced another system of service
reception at the European Championships in Istanbul (1967).
This is reception by four players (see Fig. 48). The two
setters—No. 3 in front and No. 6 penetrating—are both
available to set, and the receiving player will dig the ball to
one or other of them. When the service is high and easy to
control, No. 6 has plenty of time to penetrate and construct
the attack. In this case No. 3 is available to spike. When the
reception is less good, and the ball is dug low and fast
toward the 3-metres line, No. 3 becomes the setter. Fig. 49
shows the same system of reception when the setters are in
positions 2 and 5. No. 5 penetrates and sets whenever the
ball is dug to the left-hand half of the court.

Chapter Three: **Complex Exercises**

The first part of this book dealt with teaching methods and the way to develop them. It was suggested that due to the difficulties inherent in the various skills of· volleyball correct, logical and rapid teaching required the use of both the analytic and global methods. The resulting 'mixed' method of teaching is the one best suited to the game.

It has been emphasised that the drills should always be related to the game situation. At first, the exercise used to introduce each skill must be simple, easily performed, and not demand a great physical effort. However, as soon as the skill has been learnt, the same simple exercises (one ball between two players being the most simple) must be prolonged. The duration and the number of repetitions and the speed of performance must be increased, whilst ensuring that the least possible number of mistakes be made. This improves the performance of the skill and, most important, increases stamina. Ultimately, the player is able to perform the skill well when he is tired, a condition which may occur during a match.

Once the skill has been learnt, the coach must think of complex drills which put the player in the game situation. This involves getting the players to perform other skills before and after the skill they are practising, as is the case in any part of the game. In this way complete players are formed, able to perform all the skills well, able to use them during a game, and able to repeat them with the same precision and co-ordination throughout a match (i.e. for periods of time up to $2\frac{1}{2}$ hours).

Complex exercises have multiple aims: an improvement of one or more skills, an improvement of individual tactics and of systems of play and the development of stamina, strength and gymnastic ability. However, it would be a mistake to believe that, when a team has attained a high level, their training must be entirely composed of complex drills. Simple and complex drills must be employed at all levels, sometimes putting the accent on one and sometimes on the other. Even the world champions, East Germany and Japan, spend a large part of each training session on simple exercises for two players. This ensures that the players have the required quantity of work. Quality is obtained by expanding the simple exercises to involve other skills, other partners, and opponents as well, so that the drills come to resemble the game situation. The fact that complex drills are performed in a game situation also teaches and improves performance of the various sequences of play within the game.

In the first chapter drills were described for teaching the skills one at a time. Complex drills should relate the performance of these skills to the actions that normally precede and follow them during a game. The coach should decide on a specific number of repetitions. The drill should always be more demanding than is the same phase of the game during a match.

Complex drills can be easy or very difficult. They can comprise one difficult and one easy action, two difficult and one easy action, or several difficult actions.

The coach must be able to invent his own complex drills, related to the special requirements of his players. If he has built up a large collection of drills, he must always choose and use them knowledgeably. In the end, all depends on the coach's ability to teach. If he has this ability he will be a successful coach as soon as he has acquired enough experience. A coach who has not the ability to put his ideas across to the players, and has never had any practical experience of volleyball, cannot learn to be a coach simply by reading the best book on the game.

Those who have attended courses and have had the opportunity to hear, to see, to practise, to be corrected and to take part in extensive friendly discussions, will be familiar with the content of this book and better able to profit from it. There follows a number of complex drills which can be taken as models but also as a basis to be worked on. To get the most from the book, each teacher and coach should take the basic principles and apply them according to the standard of his team, the time the players have been training, their particular weaknesses, etc.

In all the drills that follow, the players change places and roles, after a given number of repetitions. In Fig. 1, No. 6 volleys to No. 2 and immediately runs to the No. 2 position, adopting the basic stance. No. 2 volleys and runs

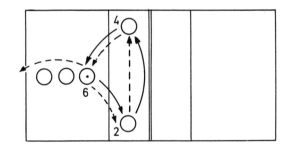

Fig. 1

to No. 4 position, and No. 4 does the same to No. 6. The drill can be made very demanding by adding other tasks—for example a dive on arriving at the new position.

Drills 2 and 3 are also practices for improving the volley. In Fig. 2 the three players at the net in court A make normal sets and the players in court B make normal and cross-court sets. Players in positions 1 and 5, each side of the net, must move quickly. Each time the ball is volleyed they should imitate the volley action, starting from the basic stance.

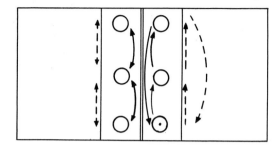

Fig. 2

In Fig. 3, the three players at the net volley to each other. At the same time, players 5, 6 and 1 run to the 3-metre line each time their corresponding front-line player receives the ball, and make a shadow volley.

Fig. 4 shows a drill for improving the dig, the volley and the placed spike. Player A spikes at C, who digs to a position in front of B. B runs forward, turns and volleys back to C, who volleys back to A. As the ball returns to A he spikes again, this time at B, who digs the ball to a position in front

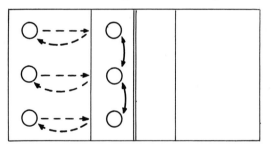

Fig. 3

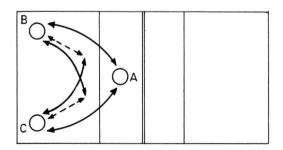

Fig. 4

of C. C runs forward, turns and volleys back to B, who volleys back to A. A keeps the exercise going by spiking again at C.

The demands of this drill can be increased by asking the players to dive after each time they play the ball. Obviously this makes the drill extremely tiring. When players can keep the exercise going for five minutes without letting the ball touch the ground, they will have reached a high technical

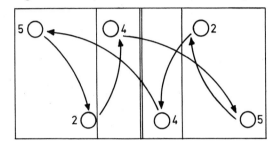

Fig. 5

standard. Once the players have got used to the exercise, the power of the spikes can be increased.

Fig. 5 shows the same drill performed on the full court with six players. No. 5 digs to No. 2, No. 2 volleys to No. 4, No. 4 spikes over the net at the opposing No. 5, who digs to his No. 2. And so on. It is important that the spikes are made at some distance from the net (one to three metres away) and absolutely necessary, if the drill is to be continuous, that spikers are able to direct their spikes.

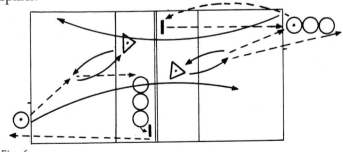

Fig. 6

Fig. 6 shows two different versions of the same type of drill. A line of players can start either from No. 2 or No. 1 positions. In court B, the player blocks, runs back to No. 1 position, volleys or digs a ball fed to him by the coach then goes to the end of the line. In court A, he blocks, serves, runs forward and volleys or digs the ball fed by the coach and then blocks again.

Fig. 7 shows a similar drill. The service can start a sequence of several actions, e.g. service, run forwards to the

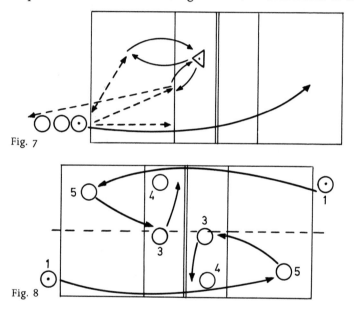

Fig. 7

Fig. 8

3-metre line, move to make a shadow dig, play the ball with a roll or dive, etc. Other variants would be service followed by three other tasks, or a number of services in succession by the same player.

In Fig. 8 the court is divided lengthways. Players are in two groups of four, No. 1 serves, No. 5 digs to No. 3, who sets to No. 4.

Fig. 9 shows a similar drill. No. 1 serves, No. 4 receives, digging to a position at the net. No. 3 runs in and sets, and

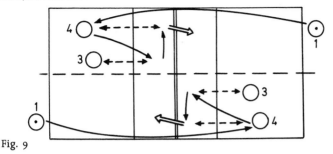

Fig. 9

No. 4 spikes. No. 1 after serving, could run in to receive No. 4's spike, or to block.

In Fig. 10, No. 1 serves, No. 4 or No. 6 receive, digging the ball to No. 3. No. 3 sets to No. 2 or No. 4, who spike, placing the ball out of reach of the server. After serving the server runs each time to a different position on his own side of the net. No. 6 always comes in to cover the spike.

In Fig. 11, No. 4 volleys to No. 3 or No. 2, who sets to him. The No. 3 (or the No. 2) then moves into position 2

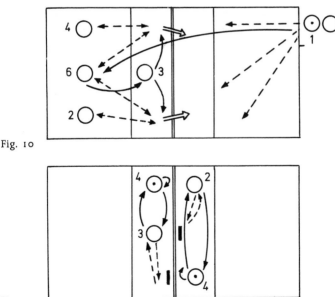

Fig. 10

Fig. 11

(or 3), blocks two or three times and then returns to his original position. Whilst the No. 3 (or the No. 2) blocks, No. 4 volleys above his own head. The exercise continues without a break. This is a particularly good exercise for the improvement or specialisation of setters. To make the drill more demanding for No. 4, he can be required to do a block each time he volleys the ball to No. 2.

In Fig. 12, No. 4 volleys to the No. 2 position. No. 2 runs in and jump sets to No. 3. No. 3 jump volleys an overhead set to No. 4. No. 4 volleys to No. 2, who has returned to a position some 5 metres from the net. No. 2 volleys back to No. 4, who jump sets to No. 3. No. 3 sets overhead to No. 2, who volleys back to No. 4 in his original position. The exercise continues without a break.

Fig. 13 shows a succession of spikes. No. 6 feeds the balls to No. 3. No. 3 sets to No. 4 who spikes, moves diagonally to receive a ball spiked softly by the coach, resumes his original position and spikes again. The exercise continues for a set number of repetitions (5 to 10).

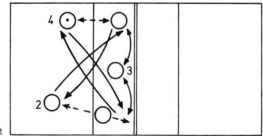

Fig. 12

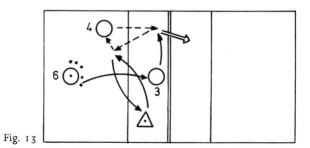

Fig. 13

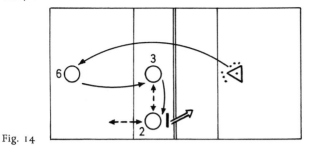

Fig. 14

Fig. 14 shows a drill involving reception, spiking, blocking and covering. The coach feeds the balls to No. 6, who digs to No. 3. No. 3 sets to No. 2 and covers the spike. No. 2 spikes and then makes a block, prior to the next repetition (5–10 repetitions).

Fig. 15 shows a drill involving spiking, setting, blocking and covering the block. The front player in line A spikes, moves to replace the setter, who replaces the No. 3 blocker, who replaces the No. 2 blocker, who replaces the

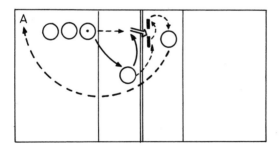

Fig. 15

player covering the block, who moves to the end of the line. The next player in the line spikes and the players move one more position. And so on.

Fig. 16 shows a continuous blocking and spiking drill. The coach and trainer volley high balls to Nos. 3 and 6. Simultaneously, the players at 2 and 4 positions (each at the head of a line of players) make a block. They then run back, in order to get a run-up for their spikes, and spike the ball set by Nos. 3 and 6. The No. 4 moves under the

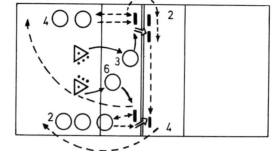

Fig. 16

net and replaces the opposition No. 2 blocker, who replaces
the No. 3 blocker, who replaces the one-man blockers in
in No. 4, who goes under the net to the end of the line of
spikers in No. 2. The No. 2 spiker moves to the end of the
line of spikers in No. 4 and the next balls are played.

In Fig. 17, the coach feeds balls across the net to No. 3
or No. 4. The ball is dug to No. 2 who either gives a jump
set to No. 3 or a long set to No. 4. Both spikers make the
spiking action. The setter sets according to the movement

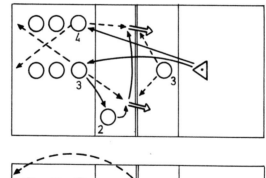

Fig. 17

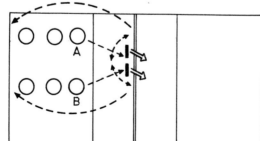

Fig. 18

of the opposition blocker No. 3, trying always to give the spiker a clear target.

The drill in Fig. 18 involves synchronisation of the block, of the approach and of the cover. No balls are used. Two lines of players, A and B. The front player in each line runs in obliquely to the net and blocks. The player from line A moves back, runs in and spikes. B covers. The players make a second two-man block, then B retreats, runs in and spikes, A covers. Finally, they make a third two-man block before returning to the back of the lines.

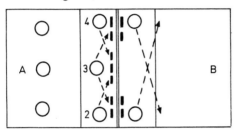

Fig. 19

Fig. 19 shows a drill for improving two- and three-man blocks, and the cover made by the front-row player who is not involved in the two-man block. The drill is performed on both courts (A and B), without balls. (i) At a signal, Nos. 4 and 3 block in position 4. No. 2 retreats to the 3-metre line to cover. (ii) At a signal, Nos. 2 and 3 block in position 2. No. 4 retreats to the 3-metre line to cover. (iii) At a signal, Nos. 2 and 4 move beside No. 3 and form a three-man block.

Several blocks can be made successively in each position. Th eplayers in court B perform the same drill simultaneously.

In Fig. 20, the coach stands on a table in court A. In court B, players stand in positions 2, 3 and 4 (a line of players in 4). Nos. 2 and 3 make a block. As soon as this block is made, the coach throws a ball into zone 2 or 3. As they land, one of the two blockers must try to set the ball to No. 4, who spikes. If necessary the set has to be made with a dive.

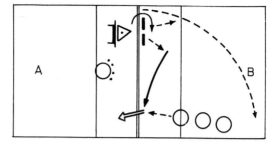

Fig. 20

Fig. 21 shows a drill without balls, to practise blocking and cover of the block. The six players adopt the defensive positions of a 3–2–1 system, as at the moment the ball goes into the opposition court. At the coach's signal, the front line of players block—either a two-man block in positions 2 or 4, or a three-man block in position 3. The back-line players, and the front-line player not involved in the two-man blocks, cover the block.

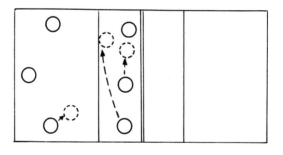

Fig. 21

Fig. 22 shows a drill to practise both defence and moving quickly into position to receive service. In court A the coach stands on a table in position 4 and spikes, or dummy spikes. A player is similarly placed in position 2 and spikes whenever the coach does a dummy. A second player is ready to serve.

In court B, the six players adopt the defensive positions of a 3–2–1 system, as at the moment the ball goes into the opposition's court. They form a block and back-court defence as the coach or the player in No. 2 position begins

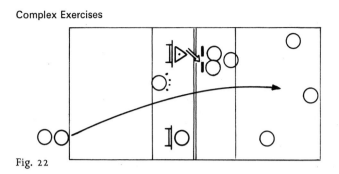

Fig. 22

to spike. At a signal from the coach, the team in court B will move from the defensive line-up, into a service reception line-up. The player in the service area then serves.

Fig. 23 shows a drill for practising the spike, the dig and the overhead volley. Two groups of three players. The first group consists of No. 1 and No. 2 in court A and No. 4 in court B. The No. 4 spikes at No. 1 who digs to No. 2, who makes an overhead volley across the net to No. 4. The second group consists of No. 4 in court A and

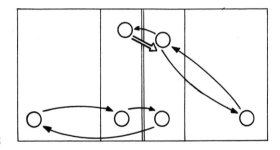

Fig. 23

Nos. 2 and 5 in court B. This group performs the same drill.

Fig. 24 shows a drill to practise penetration, digging and setting. The drill is for five players (no No. 6). No. 5 digs the ball to the net. No. 1 penetrates and sets to No. 2, 3 or 4. Nos. 2, 3 and 4 set again and the last player in the front line to touch the ball volleys it back to No. 5. Meantime, No. 1 has returned to position No. 1 and from there penetrates again to receive the ball from No. 5. The drill is performed without a break.

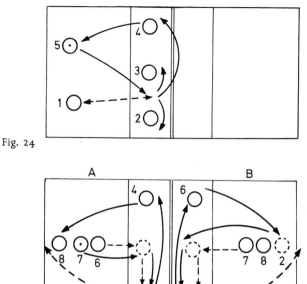

Fig. 24

Fig. 25

Drill 25 involves penetration, overhead setting and jump cross-court setting. Player 7 volleys towards the net, player 6 penetrates and volleys overhead to player 2. Player 2 makes a jump cross-court set to player 4, who volleys the ball back to player 8. Player 6 replaces player 2, who moves to the end of the line. The drill continues without a break. The position the players have reached thus far is shown on the part of the diagram labelled court B. Player 8 volleys to the net, player 7 penetrates and makes an overhead pass (in the opposite direction to the previous penetrator) to player 4, who makes a jump cross-court set to player 6 (who is in position 2). Player 6 volleys the ball to No. 2 (in zone 6). Meantime, player 7 has replaced player 4 and player 4 has moved to the end of the line. The drill continues with player 2 volleying to the net and player 8 penetrating. This drill can be performed by two groups of eight players, one group on either side of the net.

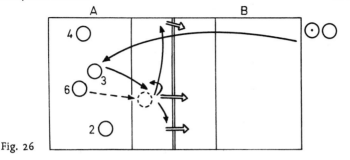

Fig. 26

Fig. 26 shows a drill for service, reception, penetration, setting and spiking. Several servers stand in court B. In court A, six players are in a reception line-up, No. 6 ready to penetrate. One player serves, No. 6 penetrates, receives the ball from the player who received service and sets to No. 4, 3 or 2, who spikes. No. 6 can be allowed to choose the spiker, or the drill can be used to practise a specific system of attack. This is repeated several times.

In order to involve other players in the same drill, three players can block or defend the back court in court B. With fewer players, the receiving team can be reduced to four: Nos. 2, 3 and 4 receiving and No. 6 penetrating.

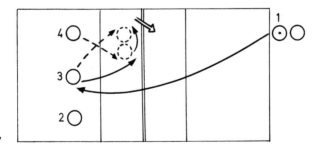

Fig. 27

In Fig. 27, three players receive on court A. Servers in court B. Service to No. 3, who digs to a mid 3·4 position at the net. No. 4 runs in and sets overhead to No. 3, who runs into No. 4 position and spikes. The same drill can be repeated with the No. 2 player running in. Spiking on the second touch can be introduced and also cross-court sets.

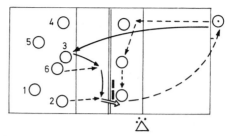

Fig. 28

In Fig. 28, six players receive service in court A. In court B, three players form two- or three-man blocks and serve (moving one position after each service). The coach stands on a table beside court B, opposite the 3-metre line.

A player serves, team A receives, and uses a system of attack; team B blocks. The coach watches the positioning of the players in team A. When a player does not cover the spike correctly, the coach throws a ball at the empty position.

Fig. 29 shows a drill, in which systems of attack and

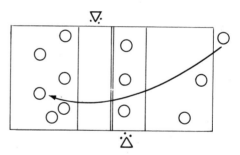

Fig. 29

defence are practised under conditions more demanding than during a match. Two teams on court. The coach and another player stand, with a number of balls each, one beside the court of each team. The players begin a game. As soon as the ball is dead, the team that lost the rally is bombarded with one or several balls at the position where the mistake was made.

Points can be counted according to the number of balls that have not been used. The team that made most mistakes

will use all the balls on its side first, and lose the competition. This drill is very demanding and requires periods of
concentration exceeding those required in a match.

A final word of advice

It is vital that you watch the reactions of your players
closely. You must learn to see from their faces whether
they can take the intense effort that you are asking from
them. At this level, it is extremely important that you do not
go too far. If you do, the best drill can produce negative
results and work against your objective.